MW01705070

AN Experimenter's Guide TO THE Full Golf Swing

Laurence E. Holt PhD

National Library of Canada Cataloguing in Publication

Holt, Laurence E. (Laurence Evans), 1940-
An experimenter's guide to the full golf swing / Laurence E. Holt.
ISBN 0-9735139-0-X

1. Swing (Golf) I. Title.

GV979.S9H64 2004 796.352'3 C2004-902080-3

Printed in Canada

Aljalar Publishing
16 Tower View Court
Lantz, Nova Scotia
Canada
B2S 1N8

E-mail: image@ns.sympatico.ca
Phone: 902 883 4433

Bookstore	$23 US	$26 CD
Mail Order	$27 US	$29 CD

Dedication

To my wife Alyce,

Who, after a highly successful competitive equestrian career, started golf in her mid-forties and by age fifty, having played less than 250 rounds of golf, earned a place on the Nova Scotia provincial senior team and competed at the nationals. She repeated this achievement a couple of years later and also won the Oakfield Ladies' Club Championships, open and senior.

Acknowledgements

Although the author is responsible for the ideas and pictures*, it took many hands and minds to complete this book. For their contributions I wish to thank:

Elliott Isenor (CPGA), Trevor Miller, Craig Slaunwhite, Ruth Maxwell, Harold White, Matt Golding, and Luke MacDonald for serving as demonstrators. Their patience and skill, often under some unusual weather conditions, were much appreciated. Jim Hoyle, Graham MacIntyre, Steve LeBlanc, Andrew Horne, Sasho MacKenzie, Merlin Comeau and Jason Holt, for editing and suggestions to improve the flow and readability of this work. Shirley Wheaton, for her deciphering, organizational and typing skills. Gary Castle for his expertise with the digital camera. Dave Grimshire, for his assistance with integrating the text and photographs. Monique Guilderson for the anatomical illustrations. Gail LeBlanc, and the graphics department at Dalhousie University for preparing and arranging the manuscript and cover layout. Finally to Dave Friesen and Hignell Books, for printing.

* Most of the Figures presented are still digital photographs based on the actual films/videos analyzed. My intention is to present clear illustrations in order to facilitate effective communication.

Foreword

Two questions immediately strike the reader. Why the title? And who is this author? No doubt you've never seen a golf book with such a strange title, and the name is not known in golfing circles. Just about all "technical" books on golf have a famous golfer or golf guru attached to them, with a simple and catchy title. This combination appears to be the path to commercial success.

It is clear that this work has neither. Why then should a golfer purchase this book? What does it offer that golfers haven't already seen or read before? These are pertinent questions that I shall now answer.

My background* is in sport science. More than 40 years of my professional life, and much of my recreational time has been spent studying human movement. The university courses I teach concern the integrative action of the nervous, muscular and skeletal systems. This is applied to all types of movement from basic exercises, resistance training and ergonomics, to virtually all sports. By utilizing electromyography (EMG), cinematography, and videography, I examine how people perform exercise and sport. I not only study human movement in the classroom and laboratory, but have enjoyed actively participating in virtually all the sports I've researched and written about. What I bring to this book is a combination of academic understanding of human movement and the practical experience of actual experimentation with the full golf swing. In fact, as members at Oakfield Golf and Country Club over the past 30 years can attest to, I continue experimenting while playing the course. I rarely stay with the same grip, stance, rhythms, patterns, and so on, more than a day or two before trying new combinations. Often I change from hole to hole, even from shot to shot. Although this is not the formula for great scoring, it has afforded me the opportunity to use all my available golf time to pursue an understanding of the full swing, and other components of the game as well. In actuality, I play relatively few rounds of golf each year, but hit large numbers of practice balls at the driving range. Occasionally I have actually performed well on the course and have recorded a number of respectable rounds (sub 80's). But I must admit that the majority of scores are above the 80 mark, often in the 90's.

* A resume appears at the back and a complete CV (curriculum vitae) is available at my website: larryholtphd.com.

My credibility then, comes from a combination of a unique academic background, laboratory experimentation, the assimilation of research done by others, and over 40 years of personal experimentation with the full swing. These are four of the reasons for the title. The fifth is that it is clear to me that the only way for each golfer to improve their swing is through experimentation. Trying to learn by the numbers, or to model a swing based on geometric positions, just doesn't work. Each golfer must fit into their unique characteristics a swing that best suits them. And although the other chapters in this book may be interesting and informative, Chapter 3 is where the action is. The swing options presented there are my suggestions for experimentation that might help each reader shape a more effective swing.

I hope that this brief explanation has answered successfully the questions regarding credibility and authorship, and that you have decided to let me help in your quest, not for "the" perfect swing, but for one that works best for you.

Recommendation

The first principle in exercise prescription is "Do no harm". My intention is to present the modifications and adjustments to the full swing that will help each golfer shape a more useful movement pattern. Although experimentation is necessary, I recommend that each time an alteration is attempted, the player go about the session in a controlled, progressive manner. Discussing each nuance with a pro/helper, using feedback wherever possible.

Should any combination of positions, movement sequences, grips, stances, etc. prove to be uncomfortable or painful, it would be wise to discontinue and move on to another approach. Any full swing that proves more effective for ball striking must be reproducible without causing injury.

A number of postural arrangements, particularly with regard to pelvic tilting, proved to be quite uncomfortable, even painful, and I've not presented them in the book. I hope that the experiments will prove helpful, and cause no injury or discomfort during the learning process.

Table of Contents

CHAPTER I

Introduction 1

The Collision 2

Collision #1 The Straight Shot 2

Collision #2 The Controlled Fade 3

Collision #3 The Controlled Draw 4

Permutations 4

CHAPTER II

The Full Swing 9

Fundamental Concepts 11

The Preparatory Phase 17

The Transition Phase 22

The Propulsive Phase 25

The Deceleration Phase (Follow-through) 32

CHAPTER III

Alternatives 34

Expectations During Stroke Modification 35

Option #1 35

Option #2 37

Option #3 40

Option #4 42

Option #5 44

Option #6 44

Option #7 55

Other Possibilities 58

CHAPTER IV

Clarification of Concepts 66

Preparatory Phase 66

Center of Mass and Right Leg/Foot 67

The Hand-Foot Concept 73

CHAPTER V

Conditioning for Golf 76

Definitions 79

Physiological Components of Fitness (General) 80

Application to Golf 80

CHAPTER VI

Improving Our Understanding of Golf 97

A Last Word 99

APPENDIX 100

RÉSUMÉ 105

CHAPTER I

Introduction

It might be safely stated that more has been written about the full golf swing than about any other movement in sport. Why this fascination with the full golf swing? What is it that drives our curiosity with regard to this apparently simple striking maneuver? One possible answer might be that in spite of the great amount of time, effort, and money expended by millions of players in an attempt to improve their play, most are disappointed by their lack of progress toward mastery of this most basic of golf's skills. Frustration is a great motivator. Intuitively we know that we are capable of striking the ball effectively, yet cannot seem to produce the needed movement patterns required for success on the golf course. Many are told that they lack the coordination to master the correct set of movements, or that they lack the proper rhythm. To most of us who have demonstrated high levels of mastery in other sporting activities, playing musical instruments, typing, or using a multitude of electronic and mechanical devices, that message doesn't ring true. We believe that the necessary qualities for an effective golf swing are there, untapped, within us. Those who have been successful at other striking activities such as baseball hitting, tennis, squash, racquetball, and table tennis, yet have been unsuccessful at golf, are perhaps the most frustrated of all. We all want to know why this discrepancy exists. The result of course, is that we search voraciously for an answer. We read everything and anything about the swing, and we constantly discuss the nuances of each article, video, and book. We watch the great players in person when we can, but more often study their movements on TV. We do all of this with the hope that one day, we will understand the "why" of successful swings and be able to apply that knowledge to our own movement patterns.

Despite our efforts, the average round of golf played by an adult golfer is nearly two strokes per hole more than the touring pro, who is often playing on much more demanding courses, and from the back tees. It has been argued that although the differences among the pros with regard to who wins a tournament might be determined by success on and around the greens, one of the major problems faced by the average golfer is focused on a full swing deficiency that leads to poor ball striking and as a result, low predictability of outcome. Many mid-, and even some high-handicap players do quite nicely on and around the greens; they simply do not know how to produce a full swing that will result in a consistently effective ball contact, which will get them to the greens in regulation.

Much confusion exists when we strike a ball and it goes to the appropriate target, then follow with the next shot that travels in a completely different path toward a most undesirable end-point. Often, we conclude that we lack a repeatable swing. If only we could reproduce the swing that got the good result, and not fall into the swing that yielded the bad shot. As we shall see later, the two movements patterns are often so close to each other that a detailed two-dimensional computer analysis could not differentiate the swings. The difference between good and bad results is extremely subtle and most difficult to ascertain, despite the commentary we often hear from analysts during telecasts of tournaments from the professional tours.

In order to more fully understand the entire process, it is necessary to have a reasonable grasp of the two constituent parts of the full golf shot. The first and most important is the collision of ball and club, for regardless of the player's swing mechanics, the nature of contact determines the flight and ultimate destination of the ball. The second component and that which produces the contact, is of course, the swing itself. This human component is the more difficult of the two to analyze, and will require considerably more time and effort before an understanding of this process emerges.

The Collision

It is interesting to note that many writers and thinkers in golf seem to agree that in spite of many swing differences all the great players make contact with the ball in a similar fashion. The principles of physics dictate that they must conform in this respect in order to hit the ball effectively. As we shall now examine, highly effective shots that accomplish the same objective can result from very different contact characteristics. Although at first this statement seems to go against basic Newtonian laws, it is in fact quite easy to demonstrate. We have all observed many fine players strike a drive and end up in a similar position on the fairway, yet the ball flight characteristics were different for each shot. A well struck high fade may carry 240 yards, hit the ground softly and bounce ahead another ten yards; a well struck straight shot may carry 230 yards and add another twenty with roll; a well struck draw may carry 220 yards and end up with the same 250 yard total. Each shot, although achieving the same goal, must have been struck differently because of the varied flight and landing patterns. This means, of course, that there are a number of successful collisions that are possible, and all that a player has to do is conform to one of these patterns.

Although there are numerous permutations, I would like to simplify this analysis by presenting 3 collisions that permit near maximum utilization of available clubhead velocity, and result in enough predictability to play an effective round of golf. Illustrations viewed from above, for a right-handed player.

Collision #1 The Straight Shot

Figure 1 illustrates the essentials of a contact that will result in a straight (or almost perfectly straight) ball flight, permitting optimum momentum transfer from clubhead to ball. This, of course, does not include extraneous forces such as wind, rain, etc. The important factors are that the clubhead is travelling directly along the intended line of ball flight and will remain in that orientation during contact, that the center of percussion of the clubhead is directly in line with the center of mass of the ball, that the ball's compression is as complete as possible (proportional to clubhead momentum), and that the face of the club is perpendicular to the intended line of flight before and during contact.

With this collision, the proper club selection for the circumstances, and the proper aim, hitting fairways and greens becomes a relatively easy procedure. It is of interest to note that many top players who hit basically straight shots are not usually among the longest of ball strikers. This, among other factors, will be discussed later.

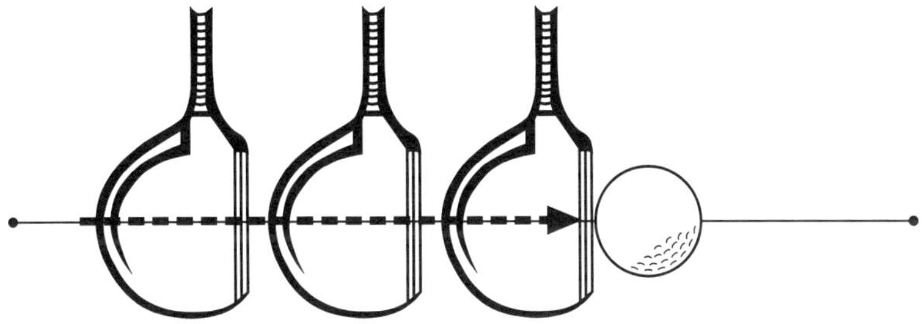

STRAIGHT SHOT

Figure 1

Collision #2 The Controlled Fade

Figure 2 illustrates the essentials of a contact that will result in a controlled fade permitting nearly all possible momentum transfer from clubhead to ball. The important factors are that the clubhead is travelling in a straight line at an angle of 5 degrees or less to the intended directional line (approaching on an outside-in path), that the center of percussion of the clubhead is directly in line with the center of mass of the ball and will remain in this orientation before and during contact, that the ball's compression is as complete as possible (proportional to clubhead momentum), and that the face is nearly perpendicular to the intended directional line of the shot. Essentially there has to be a slight obliquity between the path of the club and the face of the club before and during contact, with no change in the position of the face of the club during the contact phase. There is a small amount of friction during collision that imparts a spin other than pure backspin to the ball.

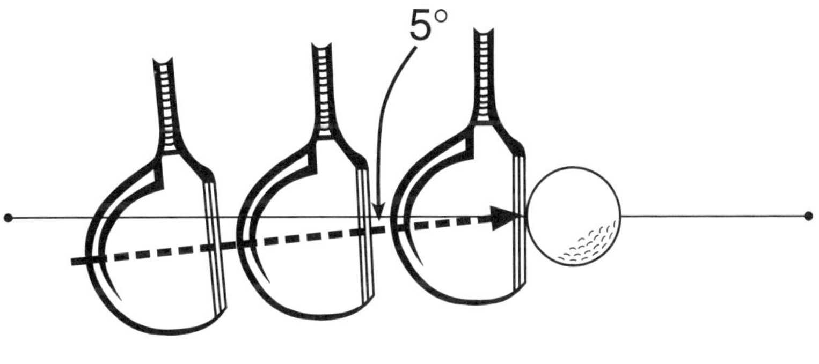

CONTROLLED FADE

Figure 2

Collision #3 The Controlled Draw

Figure 3 illustrates the essentials of a contact that will result in a controlled draw permitting nearly all possible momentum transfer from clubhead to ball. The important factors are that the clubhead is travelling in a straight line at an angle of 5 degrees or less to the intended directional line (approaching on an inside-out path), that the center of percussion of the clubhead is directly in line with the center of mass of the ball and will remain in this orientation before and during contact, that the ball's compression is as complete as possible (proportional to clubhead momentum), and that the face is nearly perpendicular to the intended directional line of the shot.

Essentially the same type of obliquity between the path of the club and the face of the club must occur (as with the controlled fade) except that the direction of approach of the clubhead has been altered. There is a small amount of friction during the collision that imparts a spin other than pure backspin to the ball. There are subtle differences between the spin imparted during the fade/draw collisions that usually results in more backspin, higher trajectory and less roll upon ground contact for the fade. However, for the purpose of this analysis these subtleties will not be discussed further. For those with a keen interest in the very complicated phenomenon that occurs with these collisions, there are many articles and some excellent books on the subject.

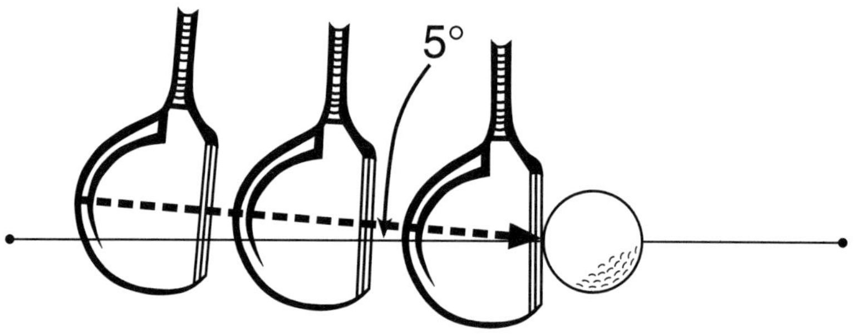

CONTROLLED DRAW

Figure 3

Permutations

Although only three collisions have been identified, there are a few permutations of these contacts that will provide slightly different ball flight paths. Essentially the variations have to do with the position of the hands when the clubhead/ball contact occurs. This factor will influence the loft of the clubface and affect the ball's ultimate flight path. The more forward the hands are during the collision, the less loft and the lower flight path. There is, of course, a small margin of error with regard to this variable, for if the hands are either too far behind or ahead of the ideal location, the loft alteration will cause a less effective outcome.

It appears then, that any of the aforementioned collisions would produce a desirable result. A straight shot that is aimed at the middle of the target area (fairway/green) will usually end up in a favorable location for the shot that follows, even if the ball is struck slightly off-center. The latter condition will result in a slight loss of distance and will land in a desirable location somewhat wide of the target.

The fade (5-15 yards for a drive, and aimed to the left edge of the fairway) will usually end up in an ideal location from which to play the next shot. Should the clubface be directly in line with the club path before and during contact a more solid collision will occur and the ball will travel in a straight line towards the left side of the fairway/green and still find a reasonably good spot from which to hit the next shot. Should it be slightly open to the intended line of flight before and during contact the ball flight will take it to the far right of the fairway/green and still leave the player with a reasonably good lie from which to play the next shot.

The same basic type of results will occur when the characteristics for the controlled draw are applied to the above situations describing the controlled fade. What is present in all the previous descriptions is that there is a larger margin for error when these collisions occur than with those demonstrated by most golfers.

Figure 4 illustrates the essentials of the classic collision of most golfers, permitting a significant momentum transfer from club to ball and a very noticeable slice to the flight path. The important factors are that the clubhead is travelling at a path angle of greater than ten degrees to the intended line of flight, that the center of percussion of the clubhead is directly in line with the center of mass of the ball, and that the clubface is perpendicular to the intended directional line. This amount of obliquity of contact will result in ball spins that will cause the ball to curve beyond the desired landing areas.

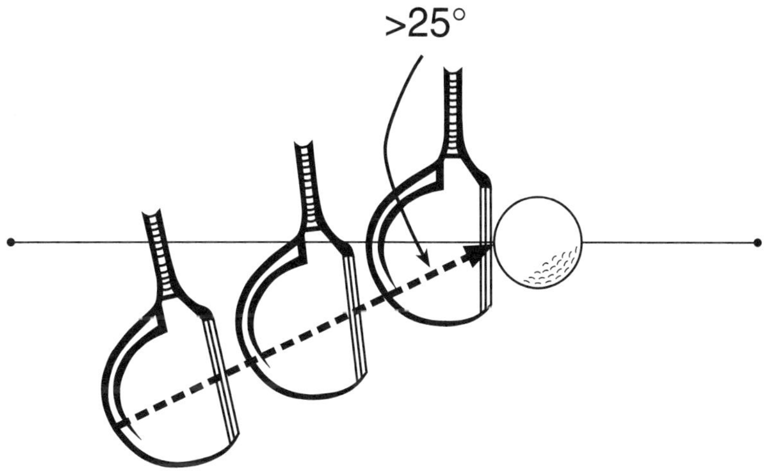

SLICE

Figure 4

This, of course, is bad enough, but the contact variations are even worse, because one (clubface perpendicular to club path during contact) leads to the ball being struck most firmly (most solid contact) and ending up either in the deep left rough or in some other trouble on the left (Figure 5); and another (ball struck slightly to the outside of the center of percussion) ends up in the middle of the fairway at a noticeable loss of distance (Figure 6). The latter shot however, is the one that confuses the most, for it is this straight shot that the player would like to have happen each and every time, even though there is a loss of distance. The player has mistakenly interpreted the situation and attributes the outcome to a better swing and club path. The resulting flight path and distance occurred as a result of the clubface opening during contact, indicating both a loss of momentum transfer and a straighter take-off path for the ball. One way of visualizing this effect is to picture a sand shot executed by a skilled player. The club path is intentionally brought across the ball from outside to inside with the clubface opened dramatically. This results in the ball taking a flight path in between the club path and face angles.

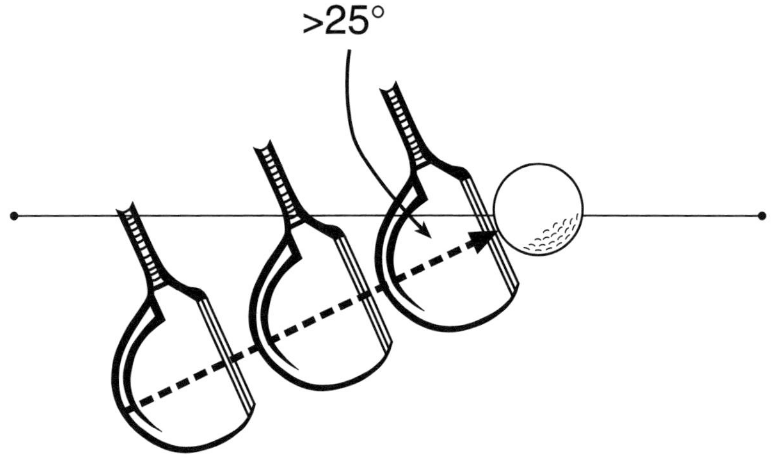

PULL

Figure 5

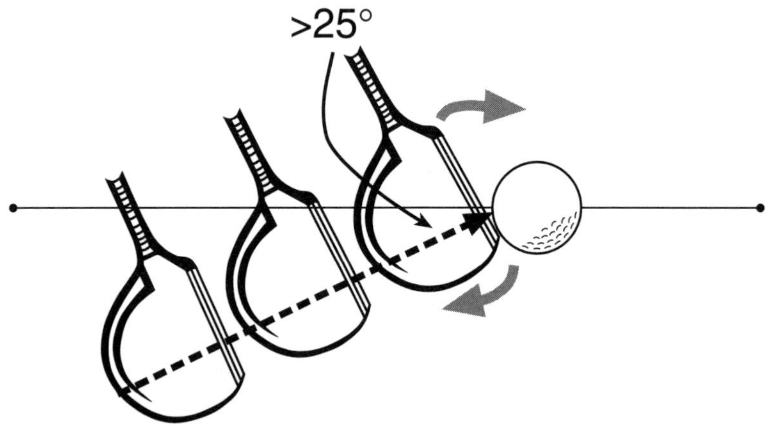

RELATIVELY STRAIGHT SHOT
(Diminished Distance)

Figure 6 Accidental Straight/Short

All three of the above examples (Figures 4, 5, 6) result from nearly identical movement patterns of the player. The major deviations in ball destinations happened as a result of minute alterations at contact. Neither visual observation, nor a two-dimensional biomechanical analysis of the player's swing, can distinguish the differences among the movements demonstrated by the player in the three shots discussed. The problem for the golfer is that s/he does not know which of the outcomes will happen or when. This level of uncertainty leads to frustration, sometimes anger, and almost always an undesirable score at the end of the round. Developing a repeatable swing is not the problem for most golfers who have been at the sport for a number of years. Lack of coordination, timing, or rhythm is not a problem for a large percentage of people who have demonstrated a well-functioning nervous system by achieving high levels of skill in other sports/activities. As we shall see, the difficulty is kinesiological, that is, restricted movement capacity at selected sites in the body, together with movement patterns that are learned in an attempt to emulate the grip, stance, and movement patterns of those more anatomically/structurally equipped for the task.

Figure 7 illustrates the essentials of a contact that will result in an excessive draw type shot permitting excellent momentum transfer from clubhead to ball. The important factors are that the club is travelling on an inside-out path of greater than ten degrees, that the center of percussion of the clubhead is directly in line with the center of mass of the ball, and that the clubface is nearly perpendicular to the intended directional line. Although there are important reasons why this type of contact is more desirable than the slice, it and its variations will also lead to the same types of problems with regard to finding and stroking the next shot. Players of this type are generally long hitters (for the velocity that they can generate), and when on their game can often score quite well. This approach to golf however, often leads to erratic scores, and is quite frustrating to the player.

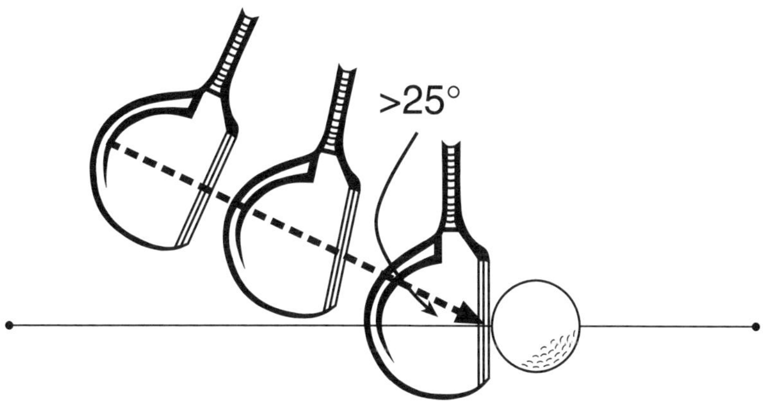

HOOK

Figure 7

The reason that the latter collision is more desirable is that it can be more easily corrected than errors of the classic type. It usually results from the player having an excessive amount of flexibility in the shoulder joints, shoulder girdle, and thoracic vertebrae. This, as we will see when the swing components are discussed, often leads the player into an undesirable transition to downswing, and culminates in the severe inside-out contact. Many great players have made the transition from excessive hook to controlled draw or even fade, and found that this enabled them to predict outcomes more effectively and thereby lower their scores.

This forms the foundation of our understanding of the golf shot itself, and will be necessary if we are to progress to the more difficult facet of this process, the full swing.

CHAPTER II

The Full Swing

One of the most fascinating works devoted to the game of golf was published over thirty years ago by Cochran and Stobbs (1969). The provocative title chosen for this book was *The Search for the Perfect Swing*. It was the first serious attempt to apply the scientific method to the full golf swing. The title itself reflects to a large degree how people within the realm of sport approach the technical aspects of their activity. There is a commonly held belief, whether it be in competitive swimming, ice hockey, track and field, equestrian, or most other sports, that there is one single best technique for accomplishing a given task. It has, in fact, been a major objective within the field of sport biomechanics to produce optimum models that represent the perfect approach to a technique. Indeed, very sophisticated computer programming that incorporates the most mathematically challenging formulae, have been produced to develop these optimization schema. They have not met with great success. Neither did Cochran and Stobbs. Why does this path of inquiry fail? The answer, I believe, lies in the diversity of human form and function. In all the sporting movements that I have analyzed through the years, all successful performers have either fallen into or learned a pattern of movement that included those factors that were *absolutely necessary* in order achieve excellence, and integrated them into their *own distinct approach* to the activity.

In philosophical terms, this is referred to as "multiple realizability." Provided the essential movements are present, success in motor skills can be achieved via a variety of unique, individualized patterns of movement.

For example, in ice hockey, differences in forward skating patterns among four of the greatest players of the past fifty years (Howe, Orr, Gretzky, Lemieux) are readily observable to the naked eye, yet all were able to generate excellent velocity when needed. How could they look that much different yet all skate so well? The key is that they all shared the required factors, yet individualized the others: trunk alignment, arm position, stroking rhythm, and so on – these varied widely. It would be more difficult to tell the differences among them should we be limited to the markings left on the ice, the range of movement at the hips, knees and ankles, or the recovery time and movement pattern of the feet. It is because these contain the required factors, those that are absolutely necessary to perform properly in order to skate at a high velocity. The same type of analysis could be applied to swimming, shooting a basketball, or any other type of sporting activity. In fact those very applications have already been made by graduate students at Dalhousie University and are described in the sport science literature.

It is my opinion that trying to apply *a single* optimization model to the general population, or to elite athletes for that matter, is a mistake. This is because the very individuals from whom the models are derived do not conform either to some theorized, mathematical elaboration, or to a model based on "averages" derived from elite players. Further, to my knowledge, there have been no controlled studies demonstrating the efficacy of this approach, or any other methodological approach to the teaching and coaching of golf. This is not unique to golf however, for there is little in the literature that supports any methodological approach to the teaching and coaching of any sport. Most of what we are told, about the proper way to teach something, is based on someone's experience and on anecdotal information. I am familiar with only one exception, that being Charles (Red) Silvia's "hand-foot concept" and its application to teaching and coaching. This method has shown itself to be effective from practical, administrative and experimental perspectives. Although we have only tested the method experimentally in the teaching of swimming, it has been applied in a practical sense in a number of different sports and has shown itself to be a superior method of instruction. It is founded on the basic principles from each of the sub-disciplines within the fields of physical education/kinesiology, including neuroanatomy, exercise physiology, biomechanics, motor learning, and applied anatomy. More on this subject will appear later.

With the millions of dollars spent on golf instruction, it would seem that research of this type should fill the literature. Each new piece of equipment, each teaching progression, or any combination of equipment and methodology should be subjected to controlled experiments where pre-test measures of swing mechanics, and more importantly actual ball flight characteristics, are compared to post-test measures. This would include hundreds of shots performed by each subject, with the distance and accuracy of each shot recorded during the experiment. An appropriate statistical analysis would then determine the effectiveness of each method or approach to instruction. Without experimentation, the process of trying to improve a player's striking ability will fall entirely on the analytic competencies, understanding of individual variances in structure and function, and communication skills of each instructor.

What will follow then, is an experimental model rather than a description of a particular method – it will be a presentation of concepts based on a set of personal experiences, an amalgamation of ideas resulting from the synthesis of kinesiological sciences, laboratory experimentation, and most importantly, the integration of this academic foundation with over *40* years of personal experimentation with the full golf swing. As mentioned in the book's Foreword, I have spent the greatest portion of my golf hours experimenting, not only on the driving range hitting thousands of buckets of balls, but on the course itself, while playing the game. Understanding through experimentation has always been my objective, and I have followed that approach throughout my work with virtually all the sports that I have analyzed and written about.

The other sources of input (academic) involved taking high-speed films and videos of the top players in Nova Scotia, computer analyzing these images, and the use of multiple linear regression to statistically analyze the data. Limited use of electromyography also added to the information pool.

This unusual combination of theoretical background, thorough review of the literature and experiments of others, personal laboratory investigations conducted at the Sport Science Lab, Dalhousie University, and over *40* years of practical stroke experimentation has enabled me to look at the full swing from a unique perspective, an experimenter's perspective in many senses. What follows will hopefully be of some benefit to the readers, not only with regard to their understanding of body movements involved in the golf swing, but also in their ability to strike the ball more effectively. It is my hope that you, the reader, will join in the experimentation as you explore the stroke options presented later in the book. That section contains suggestions that might lead to more consistent and productive shot-making. This is the basis for selecting the title of this work. It is centered on the concept of experimentation, yours and mine.

Fundamental Concepts

We all know what a full golf swing is, don't we? But before we venture into its vagaries, I believe it would be helpful to establish a workable definition. This is needed in order for us to be on the same wavelength, and will ensure that the reader has a better grasp of the material to come.

In biomechanical terms the full golf swing is considered to be a ballistic activity (the hurling or projecting of an object by means of some external force, where the object remains in motion via its own inertia.) In sports, there are obviously many examples of ballistic movements, including most throwing, kicking, and striking activities. Jumping, whether vertical (basketball, volleyball), or horizontal (long jump, triple jump), are also examples of ballistic movements. In the latter case, the body itself is the projectile, and is set in motion by means of ground reaction forces that result from the body's own internal forces.

How are these ballistic movements brought about? What do they have in common? How does this help us understand the full golf swing? By answering these questions the basis of an awareness of the kinesiology of the full golf swing will emerge.

The propulsive or striking phases of ballistic movements are multi-segmented (involve three or more body segments), and specifically sequenced (moving from larger to progressively smaller segments), requiring rapid contractions (usually concentric or shortening contractions) of the prime movers (muscles mainly responsible for the movement pattern necessary for reaching the objective.)

The rapidity of the contractions is such that the body segments themselves, once set in motion, continue moving of their own inertia, until some of their momentum (mass x velocity) is transfered to the next segment, which is lighter (less mass) resulting in greater velocity. This process continues until the smallest and last segment (in golf, the clubhead) is accelerated. This transference of momentum results from the rapid contraction of the muscle group that joins each of the contiguous segments. This is an important concept because many analysts begin from the notion that the body parts involved in the swing are simply linked together and that the kinematics (motion description) of the movement are enough to use as a basis of analysis. It is important to understand that ballistic movements, such as the golf swing, deal with the momentum of the body segments, not just their displacements.

This brief explanation of ballistic movements sets the stage for our delving into the full golf swing. The concepts presented will be clarified once the reader sees both the written and illustrative material specifically applied to the swing.

The Objective

To deliver the clubhead with sufficient velocity, proper path and correct clubface orientation, to create the desired collision, which will lead to predictable and desirable ball flight characteristics.

The Procedure

To attain the contact clubhead velocity needed in order to hit the ball the required distances, a ballistic swing pattern of movement is required for all full golf shots.

The Set-up

Holding the Club

Virtually all human activity involves use of the hands. The manner with which we shape our hands to objects and apply forces determine to a large extent how successful we are. Variations in hand (and foot) use are so important that I've included a separate section in Chapter 4 on the hand-foot concept. However, for this introductory section I shall include only basic information. The reader will no doubt be familiar with the classic grip. Figures 8-11 show the position and relationship of the hands on the grip advocated by most instructors. The club is placed between the distal heads of the metacarpals (end of palm) and the first phalanges (digits) of both hands, before the fingers and thumbs enclose the grip. Interestingly, while many professionals and low handicappers use this or a slight modification of it, it is not universally accepted as the only proper way to hold the club. A number of great ball strikers have varied from the 'classic' grip. One such variation can be seen in Figures 12-15, where the club is placed more in the palms before closing the fingers around the grip. Another variation can be seen in Figures 16-19 where the club is placed almost entirely in the fingers. Since many combinations are possible, experimentation is necessary in order for each golfer to find their best grip.

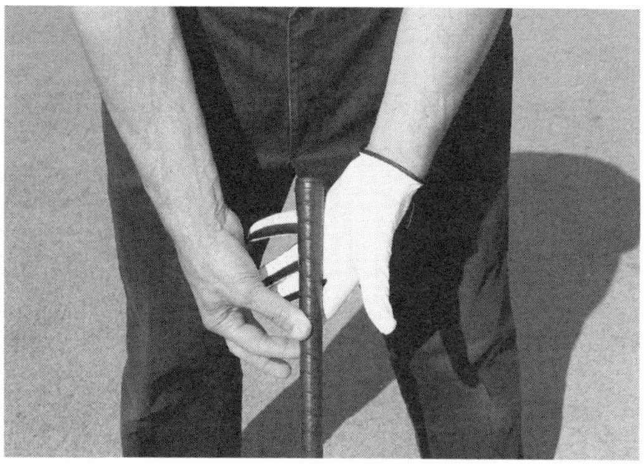

Figure 8

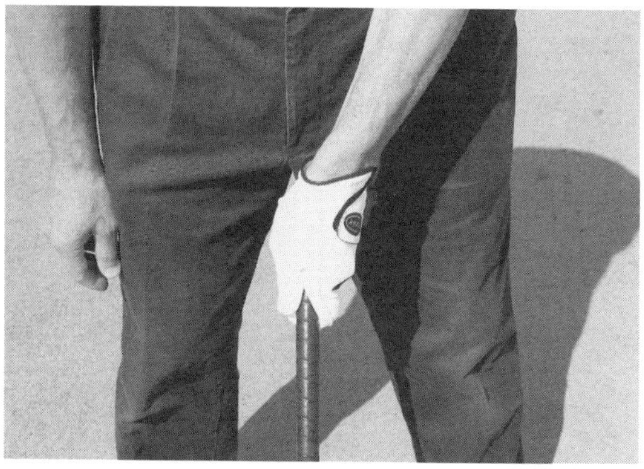

Figure 9

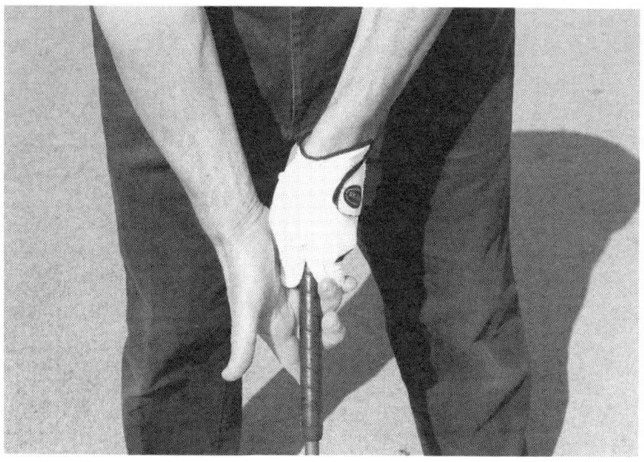

Figure 10

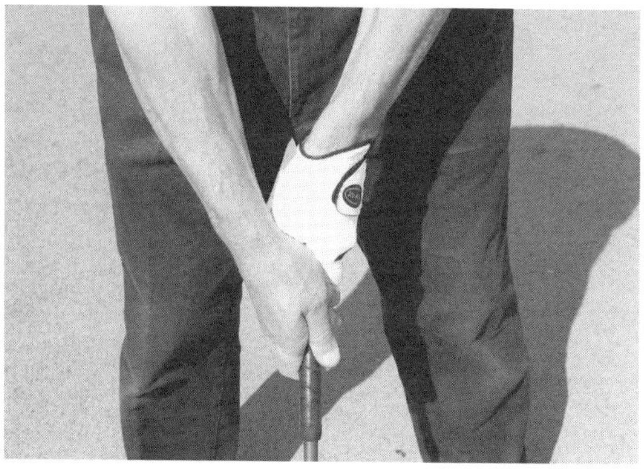

Figure 11

Conventional Grip

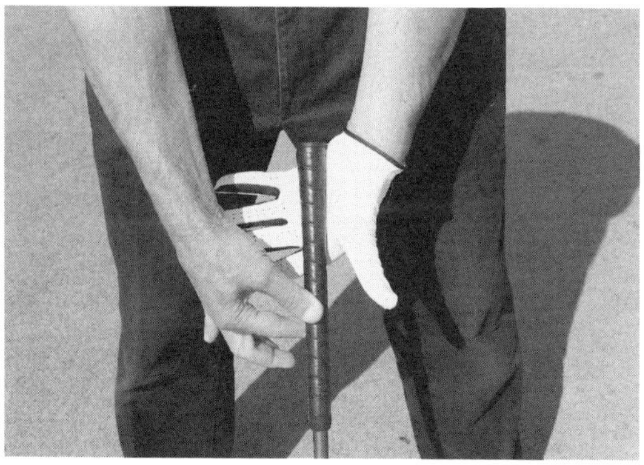

Figure 12

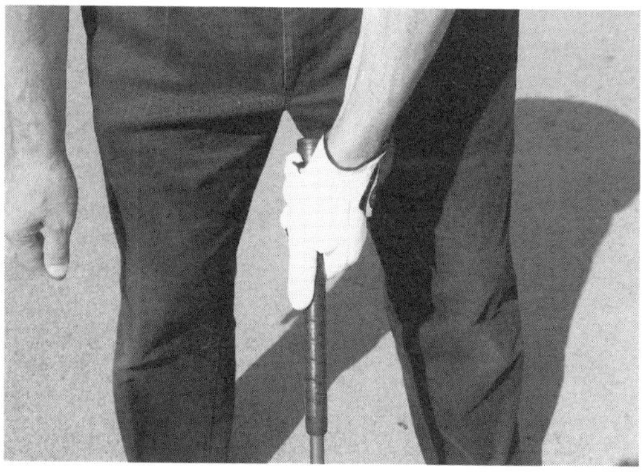

Figure 13

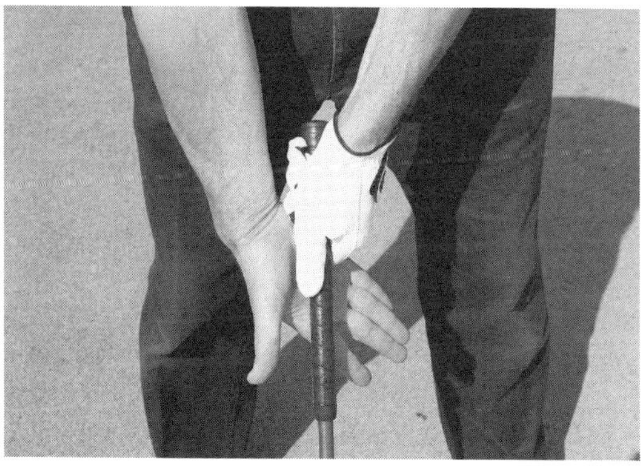

Figure 14

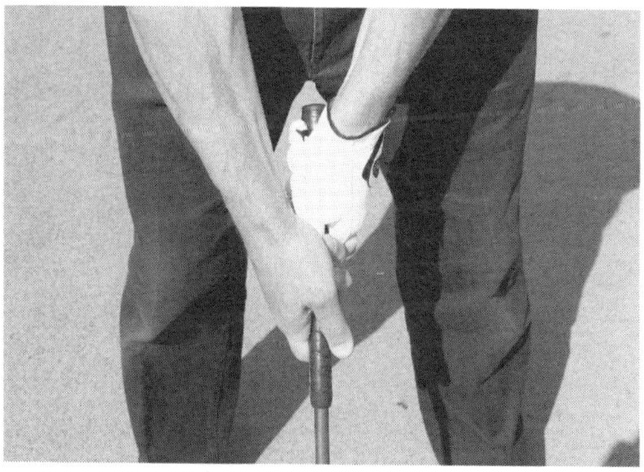

Figure 15

Palm Grip

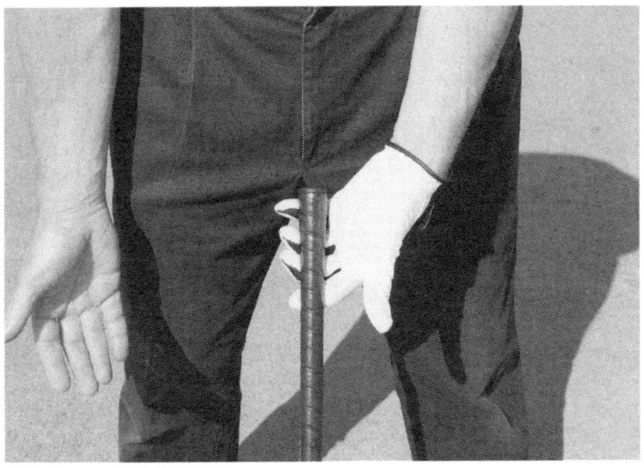
Figure 16

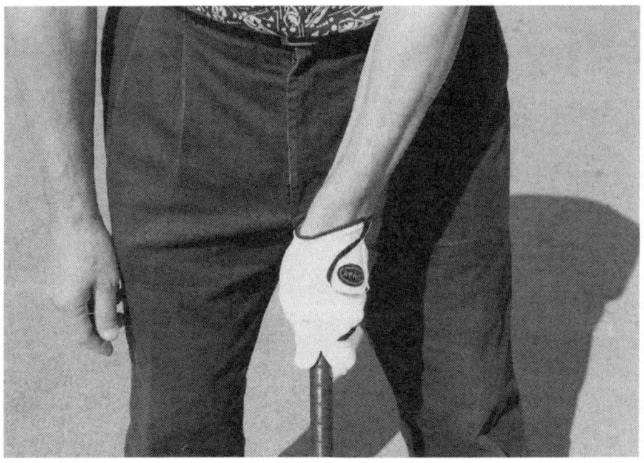
Figure 17

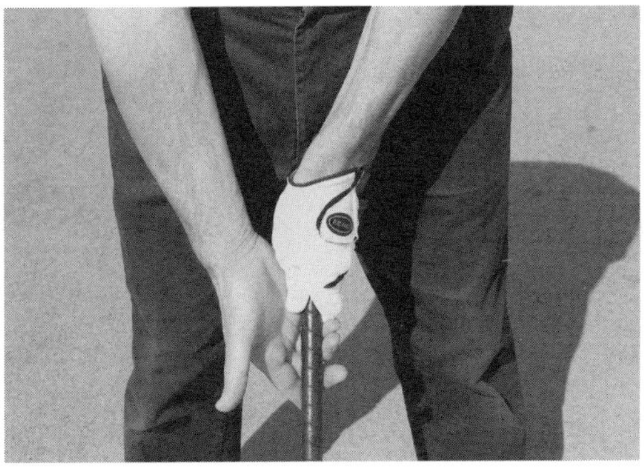
Figure 18

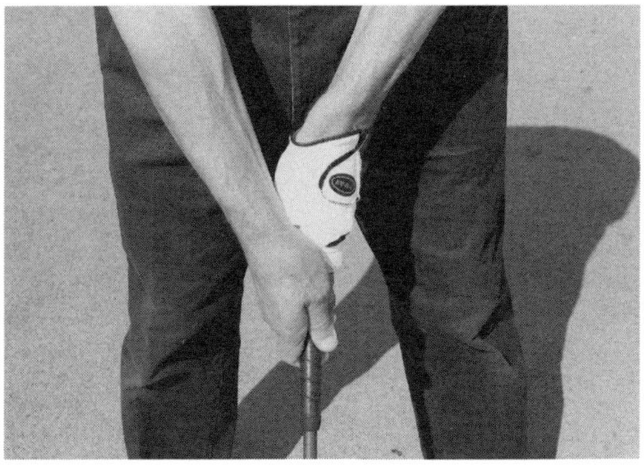
Figure 19

Finger Grip

Figure 20

Figure 21

Stance/Posture

Because the ball is motionless each time we strike it, we have the opportunity to position our body as we like prior to initiating the swing. This position should allow for all body segments to contribute effectively to the swing. Figures 20 and 21 show a traditional stance, posture, and ball position used by many excellent ball strikers when hitting with a driver.

Keep in mind that most of these prodigious ball strikers are kinesiologically different from average individuals, particularly with regard to thoracic mobility. Figures 22-27 show this difference. It could very well be that the stance/posture of these successful ball strikers is inappropriate for most average players. More discussion appears in Option #6 later in the book.

Figure 22 Average Golfer

Figure 24 Long Driving Competitor

Figure 23 Average Golfer-Thoracic Rotation (30°)

Figure 25 Long Driving Competitor Thoracic Rotation (80°)

Figure 26 CPGA Pro-Long Driver

Figure 27

In Figures 20 and 21 the head and neck are flexed, that is, angled slightly forward. The chest (thorax) and pelvis are also angled forward. This movement takes place between the pelvis (anterior tilt) and femurs, resulting in a small amount of hip flexion. The knees are slightly flexed, and the ankles in slight dorsi-flexion. The arms are raised a few degrees away from the vertical, with both scapulae depressed. The feet are approximately shoulder width apart, the right perpendicular to the target line, the left turned outward. The position of the shaft of the club relative to the left arm results in a nearly straight alignment. The left wrist is in a neutral or slightly flexed position.

Although this approach is the overwhelming favourite of most teachers, it, like the grip, is not universally accepted as the necessary foundation of the full golf swing. Of the modifications possible, Figures 28 and 29 represent the stance/posture that goes with the palm grip (Figures 12-15) mentioned above. This will look familiar to many readers as the approach advocated by "natural golf" instructors. Since many golfers have experimented with this, and other stance/posture/grip combinations and found success, it seems that even before the swing has begun, much experimentation is necessary in order to find each individual's best set-up.

Figure 28

Figure 29

Phases of the Full Golf Swing

The following analysis of the full, right-handed golf swing will be subdivided into four phases: preparatory, transition, propulsive, and follow-through. Because there are so many possible patterns of movement to accomplish these phases, our focus will be on those elements that are absolutely essential, with important variations discussed in order to clarify successful alternatives to the traditional model, which will be discussed later.

The Preparatory Phase

Each swing has a first movement. For some it starts by drawing or pushing the club directly away from the ball after the address position has been assumed. For many, a "trigger" mechanism is employed before the club is moved away from the ball that enables the golfer to initiate the preparatory pattern in a predictable and useful manner. It usually involves either a slight weight shift via muscle activity in the lower half of the body or a slight rotation of the head and neck. Although not essential, many excellent ball strikers have found this to be a valuable component of their swing pattern. Option #6 (Bobby Jones) contains an example of how this works effectively.

There are two common preparatory elements whose performance is necessary for a player to deliver the required ballistic striking motion. They are usually accomplished within the same series of movements, and are the components of what is generally referred to as the back swing. (I prefer to use the term 'preparatory movement', as it enables one to discuss any ballistic activity with the same term.)

Figure 30

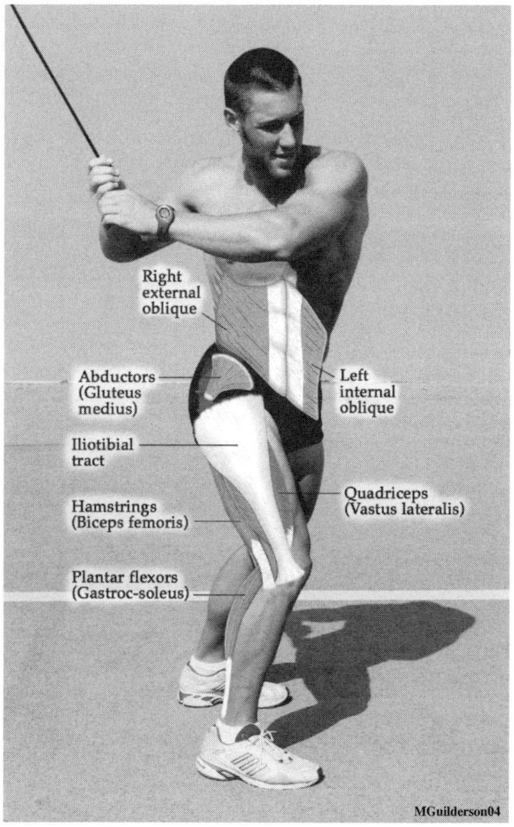

Figure 31

Figure 32

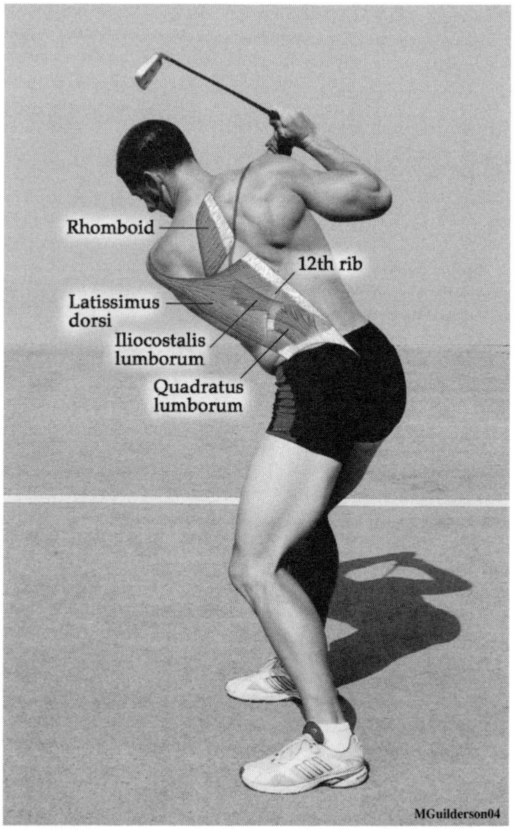

Figure 33

Figure 34

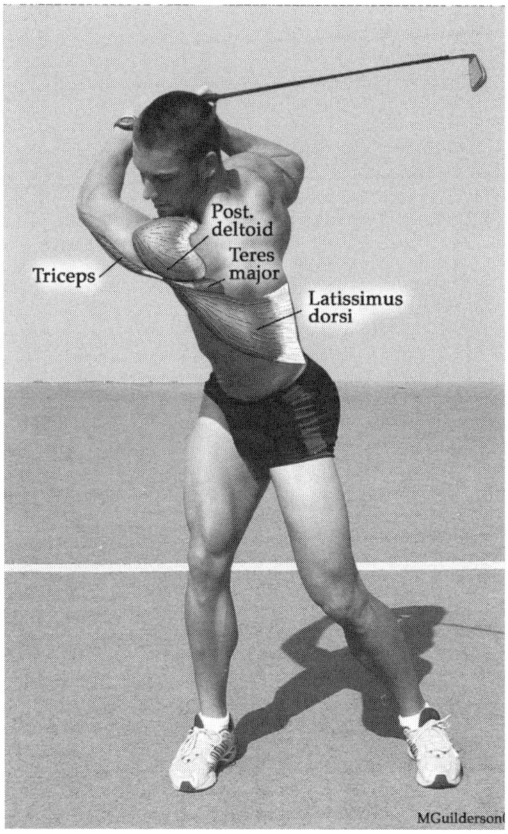

Figure 35

Element #1 — A series of movements places all possible contributing body segments in the most advantageous position for contributing to the momentum transfer necessary for reaching the desired clubhead characteristics at contact. This involves the loading of muscles of the right lower quadrant of the body, and the placing of all significant upper body prime movers in a lengthened or stretched position at the appropriate time (Figures 30-35). By the latter process, the contributing muscles that rotate the trunk to the left around its long axis, adduct the left scapula, horizontally abduct the left shoulder joint, extend the left elbow, and ulnar flex both wrist joints, are able to generate more instantaneous power than would be available to them in an unstretched position. (This stretching of tissue includes not just the muscle itself, but the surrounding fascia which plays a key role in both the amount of stretch achieved and the resulting force of contraction).

Element #2 — The above movements result in a temporary, nearly complete unweighting of the left or lead foot. Many excellent players achieve this objective with a very small shift in the body's center of mass toward the right leg/foot. Usually this is done by those with a very fast preparatory phase (Figures 36 and 37). The bend in the shaft at take away, caused by an inertial lag in the clubhead, indicates a forceful initiation of the backswing.

Figure 36

Figure 37

Others achieve this objective by means of a considerable shift in their center of mass (5-6 inches or more), and this is usually accomplished with a slower preparation phase (Figures 38 and 39). The timing, the amount of the unweighting, and the distance of center of mass movement vary considerably among elite players. The time required to achieve these two elements and the manner in which the player goes about this unweighting is of critical importance, and will be discussed more fully later in this section. In fact, as we observe the professionals playing on tour it is obvious that they all prepare for the striking phase using widely different movement sequences, patterns, and rhythms. They all, however, achieve the two required preparatory objectives.

A most important question to ask at this point is, how should any one golfer perform the preparatory movements, given that the best in the world do not conform to any standard? Further, if they don't conform to a standard, is it helpful to attempt to learn the traditional backswing? It is my view that most golfers actually hinder their possibilities at good ball striking by trying to conform to traditional methods of learning the backswing. By moving with a controlled, slow backswing tempo and artificially achieving certain clubhead, hand, arm, and shoulder positions at various stages of the backswing, the average person inevitably has an incomplete unweighting and/or places certain body segments in undesirable positions, stretching muscle groups that will interfere with the proper execution of the striking phase. This is not often appreciated during lessons because the movements are usually done slowly, and are followed by a slow controlled downswing. This approach, as many of you have experienced, works well when the objective is to hit the ball at half speed or less. It fails

Figure 38

Figure 39

when you actually want to strike the ball as it needs to be struck during the actual playing of the game. Most golfers do not understand the differences that exist in the delivery system when the player changes from a controlled traditional full swing to one which places a complete stretch on the major muscles, necessary in order to achieve enough of a backswing to apply the needed acceleration to the clubhead, for the length of shot desired.

After a discussion of the transition and striking phases of the full swing, I will discuss why the traditional backswing sets the average golfer up for failure. As well, I will suggest two alternatives to the traditional backswing. It will, however, necessitate a good deal of experimentation under the watchful eyes of a teaching pro, or someone with a keen analytic ability, to determine which alternative is best for you. Make no mistake, for most of us, the relearning of such a complicated procedure is no easy task, even if you understand the concepts.

Any successful preparatory phase accomplishes the two required elements. This is necessary in order for the player to bring about a desirable transition and the initiation and execution of a successful ballistic striking phase. The backswing must fit each individual's unique characteristics, in order to enable the player to accomplish the desired objectives without setting up additional segment positions that will lead inevitably to ineffective shotmaking. It will be seen later that one characteristic flaw that often occurs, involves the positioning of the pelvis as it relates to both hip joints, shoulder girdle, and thorax (chest). Both the extent and the timing of this flaw constitute one of the common mistakes of most unsuccessful ball strikers. A second key error is the movement pattern of the shoulder girdle during this phase. Both will later be discussed in detail.

The Transition Phase

At some point, the preparatory phase becomes the propulsive. For many effective ball-strikers the preparation of all body segments comes to a stop; there is no further shifting of the center of mass to the right, and the hitting phase is initiated by a sequential reversal of movement (Figures 40 and 41).

Figure 40

Figure 41

For the majority of effective ball-strikers there is a more noticeable transition phase, which is characterized by the reversal of movement of the lower body (legs and pelvis) with either a continuation of the preparatory movements of the arms and hands, or a delay in the initiation of the propulsive phase of the arms and hands (Figures 42-44).

Figure 42 Backswing

Figure 43 Early Propulsive Phase

There are two elements that characterize a successful transition. This phase starts when the partial or complete unweighting of the left side stops (Element #1). It ends when the left hand begins to reverse its direction, (Element #2). For both types the successful unweighting leaves the body with little or no support from the left foot. As a result, gravity begins moving it to the left, the beginning of the propulsive/striking phase. This all takes place during the transition in order to stretch the upper body prime movers more completely. With most average golfers, who are ineffective ball-strikers this phase may be characterized by either a shift of the center of mass to the right side (normal procedure) followed by a reversal to the left to begin the striking phase, or by the dreaded "reverse weight shift", which arises because

Figure 44

the preparatory movements failed to cause an unweighting of the left leg to begin with (Figures 45 and 46).

Figure 45

Figure 46

In either case the average player's transition to downswing usually consists of a unified, horizontal body rotation (involving pelvis, trunk, and shoulders) and a horizontal reversal of hand direction with the well-known problems that result. The disastrous transitions common to the average player are the result of backswings that leave the golfer no possibility for alteration of a fully ballistic swing, and the only recourse, should some semblance of control be the outcome of the shot, is to slow the transition, and continue to slow the striking phase, thereby lessening the outside-in club path. Of course, under these conditions, the ball may be struck properly but with greatly diminished momentum, and will have a very short flight. Either approach is unacceptable to most golfers, for in the first instance there is greater clubhead velocity with low predictability and often undesirable outcomes, and in the second there is higher predictability but lower clubhead/ball velocity. Average ball strikers are always in conflict. They know intuitively that a full ballistic swing is necessary to develop the needed clubhead velocity, and that they can indeed bring about a sufficient amount of clubhead speed, yet they also know, all too well, what occurs when they perform a full ballistic striking motion.

The most important characteristic resulting from the backswing and transition is the effect these factors have on the path of the hands at the beginning of the downswing. *Studies at our lab have shown that 80% of the variance in the quality of full golf shots can be predicted by one simple measurement, that being the path of the hands during the first foot of the propulsive phase of the swing* (Figure 47). From the classic position at the top, if the hands move more horizontally than vertically during this critical time, then the outcome will be undesirable. The greater and faster this horizontal component is, the worse the effect. This factor will be the focus of the next section which deals with the striking/ propulsive phase of the swing. One exception to this concept is described in Option #6, where the hands move horizontally, but from a deeper "set" position.

Figure 47

The Pr opulsive Phase

Although the line between transition and propulsion is sometimes difficult to isolate, the seven common elements that are necessary for an effective propulsive/striking phase are clear. They are: vigorous push with the lower right quadrant, initiating the phase (Element #1), a more vertical than horizontal path of the hands from the transition to downswing (Element #2), a sequential transfer of momentum from larger to smaller segments (Element #3), the hands moving in two dimensions (planar) when they are being accelerated by the movement at the left shoulder joint (Element #4), the clubhead as a result of the final wrist/hand movement being set on one of the accepted paths (Figures 1-3) as it approaches the ball (Element #5), the clubhead being stabilized as it approaches the ball with no acceleration during the final foot or more prior to contact (Element # 6), and clubhead/ball contact being clean and in the center of percussion (Element # 7).

The initial unweighting process not only brings gravity into play, but also forces both the body's weight and its momentum onto the right leg/foot. This "loading" of the right side enables the golfer to initiate a vigorous force against the ground by contracting many of the loaded muscles of the right hip, thigh, shank, and foot. Although the interactive ground reaction force drives the body's center of mass to the left, it does this by influencing primarily the lower half of the body. The greater the golfer's trunk flexibility (Figures 22-27), the more movement of the lower anatomy, resulting in a greater lengthening of the prime movers of the trunk. This is the first part of the propulsive phase and creates a large momentum by moving the more massive parts of the body (particularly for those with large legs and pelvis, less so for leaner individuals) in the desired direction of the swing (Figure 48).

Figure 48

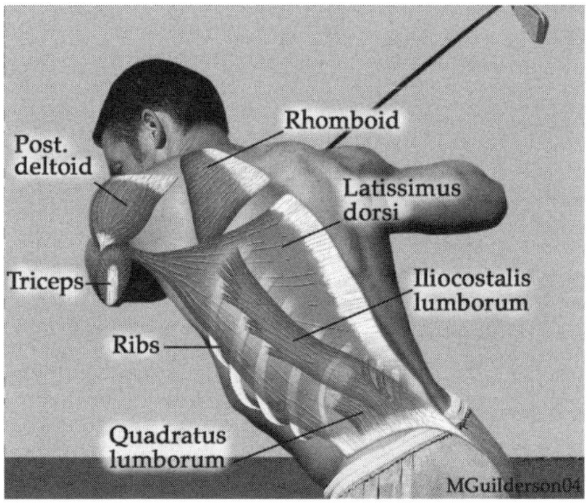

Figure 49

If this movement is more lateral than rotary it accomplishes two very important objectives. The first is that it further stretches the prime movers of the trunk (left quadratus lumborum, iliocostalis lumborum), shoulder girdle (left rhomboids), shoulder joint (left latissimus dorsi and left posterior deltoid), and elbow (left triceps). These muscles are illustrated in Figure 49.

The second, which is of great importance, is that the hands are directed more vertically than horizontally during the initiation of the propulsive phase. It is not necessary for the golfer to do this consciously, rather it is the result of the movements performed by the lower body. This is explained by Newton's third law, the action of moving the connecting link between thorax and legs (pelvis) to the left causes an equal and opposite reaction driving the chest and parts connected to it in the opposite direction (Figure 48 - Hinged Rulers). This occurs while the thorax is rotating toward the intended direction of the shot around the long (vertical) axis. In addition, there are many variations of this initial phase that all lead to effective ball striking. These hand paths can be seen in Figure 50. They are examples of excellent hand movement patterns.

The first part of an effective striking phase has seen the lower body move to the left, along with some pelvic rotation about the hip joints creating a large momentum and causing the hands to move more vertically than horizontally from the transition. This movement has placed the prime movers of the next segment (thorax/chest) in an extreme stretch, and as a result these prime movers are now capable of high levels of instantaneous power when they

Figure 50

Figure 51

are signaled to contract (shorten). The effect of these muscular contractions is threefold: it accelerates rotation of the trunk, stretches the prime movers of the left shoulder girdle and left shoulder joint, and decelerates the lower body (Figure 51). Because the quadratus lumborum, iliocostalis lumborum and the latissimus dorsi muscles are attached to the posterior pelvis and sacrum, a portion of the momentum created by the lower body can be transferred to the next segment to which these muscles are attached and add to the overall effect of the swing.

For the average golfer, the body positions at the transition usually involve a significant amount of pelvic rotation. This is necessary in order to accomplish a complete backswing. Figure 52 illustrates a typical transition position for an average player.

It is important to understand just what is occurring in Figure 52. The golfer has started from a traditional set up, with the head and neck flexed and the trunk angled forward. Due to a limited amount of combined movement capability in the shoulder joints, shoulder girdle, and chest (thoracic vertebrae and attachments), this golfer must complete the preparation by creating additional pelvic rotation. This is accomplished by continuing to apply force to the ground with his left leg/foot, and by pulling back with his right arm (adduction of the right scapula and horizontal abduction of the right shoulder joint). This latter motion is part of the preparatory phase of most throwing activities, and is automatically performed to position the right side for the ballistic throw which is to follow. However, in doing this, the golfer has created a most undesirable situation, which includes five characteristics:

1 — solid contact of the left upper arm with the chest, 2 — elevation of the left scapula, 3 — excessive pelvic rotation (actually a pronounced internal rotation of the right hip joint, external of the left), 4 — some trunk extension and lateral sway, 5 — left hip and knee flexion which may cause the left heel to raise from the ground (not indicated.)

Figure 52

This combination not only moves the entire trunk away from its original alignment, it also locks the player into a position from which there are but two options, slow the striking phase to diminish the horizontal path of the hands at the transition to downswing (which leads to the outside-in clubpath), or release with a full swing (which leads to the undesirable consequences previously described.)

Why is this inevitable? The simple answer is that there is no "give" in the system. The outward rotators of the right hip joint are fully stretched, the thorax is locked onto the pelvis, the left scapula is elevated, the left shoulder joint and arm are locked onto the thorax and the golfer cannot initiate movement of the pelvis without affecting the hands (moving them horizontally to start the striking phase). Although this is bad enough, a number of golfers add more difficulty to the process by failing to unweight the left side during the preparation phase. This results in a loading (stretching) of the internal rotators of the left hip joint which, when they contract, add to the already undesirable horizontal spinning of the pelvis, and causing the center of mass of the body to move to the right. Even if the golfer does successfully unweight most of the left side, the position illustrated loads the extensors of the left hip and knee, which leads to contracting at the transition to downswing. This causes the left hip joint to move backwards, resulting in an additional force contributing to the "spinout" of the pelvis.

Not only is the club "cast", but the die also. For the result of this typical approach to the golf swing is the unpredictability of the actual contact and consequent ball flight. For the average golfer the remainder of the striking phase that follows the spinout basically consists of the release of the hands, and the resulting acceleration of the clubhead. *It must be remembered that all this has resulted from the player beginning the swing from a traditional set-up and grip. It will be seen later in Option #6 that for a number of golfers this problem may be corrected with a more upright trunk alignment and a different pattern of motion.*

For the fortunate golfer whose hand path is favorable for achieving the desired ball contact, the continuation of the striking phase will now be discussed. The trunk rotation has further stretched the muscles of the shoulder girdle, shoulder joint, and elbow, which are then stimulated to contract, causing the final acceleration of the hands. This uses up some of the trunk's momentum and results in its deceleration. Figures 53 and 54 illustrate this part of the striking phase.

Figure 53

Figure 54

The final movement that causes the clubhead to attain its greatest acceleration involves release of the hands by means of a wrist movement termed ulnar flexion (both wrists perform the same action). Figures 55 and 56 demonstrate this combined motion, which incidentally is similar to the movement used to accelerate other implements such as baseball bats, fishing rods, etc.

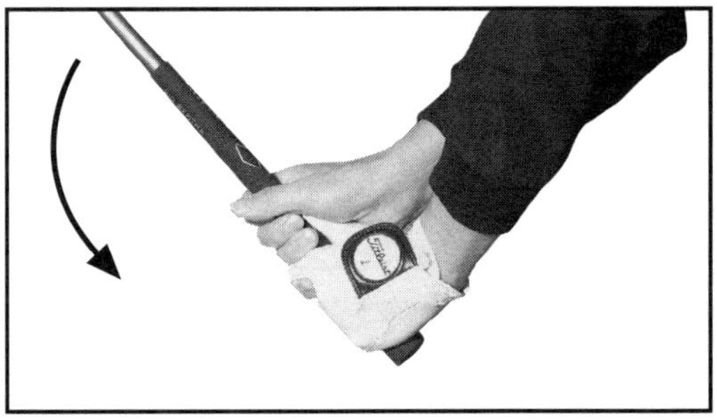

Figure 55 Wrists radially flexed

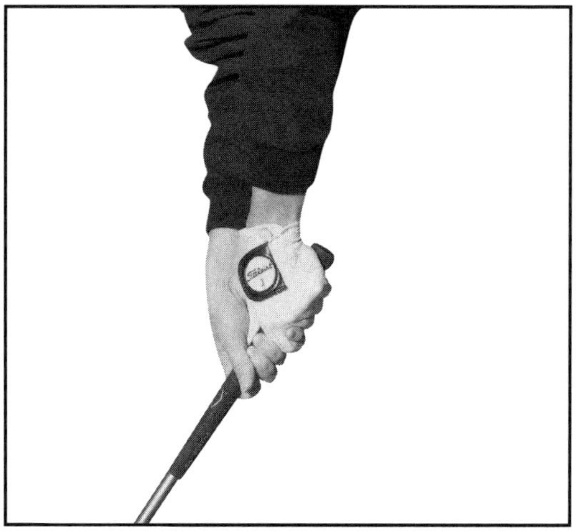

Figure 56 Ulnar flexion completed

Ulnar flexion takes place even when the right wrist joint (or both wrists) are hyperextended. Few golfers can maintain a "neutral" angle with both wrists at the top of the swing.

It is important to understand that this is the last time the golfer can effect a change in the clubhead before contact is made. For better ball strikers ulnar flexion is performed while the hands are moving in a linear (planar) fashion. If they are moving in a three-dimensional pattern, such as performed by the average player, the control of contact characteristics is extremely difficult. The speed of the hands during their acceleration phase (Figure 53) is very high (with a small portion due to gravity), and when the ulnar flexors are caused to contract violently the clubhead is accelerated to such an extent that it is travelling so fast that any additional muscular contraction could not possibly affect its course. The clubhead, in a sense, becomes ballistic for a short period of time, from ulnar flexion, when it has its greatest acceleration, to ball contact, where hopefully it decelerates as much as a true center hit demands (Figure 57). The momentum in the arms and hands is reduced in proportion to the force of muscular contraction that brings about the ulnar flexion. After contact the remaining momentum in the clubhead is then sequentially taken back by the body, which results in the follow through. In dealing with acceleration/momentum either in the preparatory, transition, propulsive, or follow-through phases, I do not intend to suggest that all the momentum from each segment is taken up by the succeeding segment. Rather, a portion is usable, and that depends on the individual, their technique, body type and segment masses.

Figure 57

If one were to hit an object large enough to take up all the momentum of the body-club system, then all movement would come to an abrupt halt, with rather jarring consequences for many of the soft tissues of the body. That is why practice drills that emphasize hitting into large objects such as tires, bags, and so on, must be done with caution. In considering that such practices would have no beneficial effect on actual ball-striking, it is my belief that they should not be done at all.

There has been a belief espoused in golfing circles that pronation of the right forearm is accomplished by conscious motor control prior to the club making contact with the ball. I do not believe this is correct. The closing of the clubface is due to the hosel connecting the shaft and clubhead, and the stabilization of the head occurs during the final path of the clubhead toward the ball. *Again, the clubhead should not be accelerating up to ball contact, but rather should have reached its terminal velocity well before the contact point.* Our studies indicate that the clubhead is "floating" into contact for more than a foot prior to collision, and that it is in this interval that the clubhead wobble is stabilized and the face is undergoing little change in its position.

There are three misconceptions that seem to be emphasized by some teachers: that acceleration should continue up to contact, that an attempt be made to accelerate through contact, and that pronation adds this final acceleration. It seems irrational to want the clubface to make contact with the ball at an exact angle each time while changing that angle significantly right up to the point of contact. Because of the point of attachment of the shaft to the clubhead, any forces acting through the shaft must change the orientation of the face dramatically up to contact. This would make it extremely difficult for even the most talented golfer to effect a consistent and desirable collision. The technical changes that lower the head torque help with this problem somewhat, but it is clear that a more effective approach is to accelerate the clubhead in order have maximum velocity reached a considerable distance before contact, for the clubhead to be stabilized prior to collision, and for maximum deceleration to occur as a result of the best possible contact.

The Deceleration Phase (Follow-through)

The deceleration phase has one function, the dissipation of the remaining momentum contained in the club and body segments. This momentum, if spread over time and distance, will enable the player to finish each full swing without injury. Because of the forces applied against the ground by the right leg/foot at the start of the propulsive phase, the entire body's motion is toward the left foot, and the unused momentum causes the majority of the body weight of most great ball strikers to come to rest over the left foot at the termination of the swing (Figure 58). There are exceptions to this, most notably Moe Norman, Walter Hagen, and others who used a very wide stance throughout the swing. This approach restricts excess pelvic movement and makes it easier to control and repeat swing mechanics. However, it makes a full transfer of weight to the left foot less likely.

Figure 58

Figure 59

Although there are some who teach that there is one optimal end point position, this seems unreasonable, when one observes players on the professional tours. There are many variations to the termination of the swing. However, as long as the weight is primarily on the left side, and the player is not compromising the soft tissues of the body, then the termination phase is acceptable. Width of stance, leftover momentum, club path to contact, elasticity of the tissues absorbing the momentum will all result in individual variation in the follow-through as they do in the other phases of the swing. Finishing fully on the left side is not actually required. Perhaps the best ball-striker in the game's history, Moe Norman, finished his swing with a lower percentage of his weight on the left foot that most other professionals (Figure 59). At the other end of the continuum, it seems that it is not even necessary to stop the forward momentum at all. Gary Player often used a striking method such that the termination phase momentum carried over into his post-shot fairway walk. It should be kept in mind, however, that striking the ball effectively, and not injuring the body, are the objectives, not looking great at the finish.

Summary

There are two important reasons why experimentation with the grip, stance, set-up, initiation (trigger), and completion of the preparatory phase are all of great importance. The first is that they determine the path of the hands at the transition to downswing, which is the crucial component of the golf swing. The second is that these elements are either performed with no time constraints (grip, stance, set-up), or are performed at speeds that are more readily under conscious control, (backswing). The acceleration of the hands during downswing which is brought about by the body's movements, is performed ballistically, as is the acceleration of the clubhead. These latter components are pre-programmed into the swing, and are not easily altered during their execution.

Chapter III involves a number of possible swing options that will aid the golfer in developing a more vertical transition movement, causing the hands and club to move through one of the acceptable paths to contact.

CHAPTER III

Alternatives

Although brief, and simplified, I hope that the material to this point has been informative, and has led readers to question previously held notions regarding the full golf swing. I realize however, that most readers have come to this point, not so much with the goal of understanding more about the swing, but with the hope of making constructive changes to their swings in order to play the game more effectively.

What follows is a series of suggestions for change that are based primarily on my own experimentation with the full golf swing. I have no laboratory research data upon which to base these suggestions. In addition, I am not a golf professional. In fact I have never taught an official golf lesson to anyone. These alterations are presented with the hope that they might be helpful to those who have tried on other occasions to improve their striking ability, but have not experienced much success.

I have personally tried virtually all permutations of grips, stances, postures, backswings and downswings. The members at Oakfield Golf and Country Club, Oakfield, Nova Scotia, can readily attest to the many hours, days, and years of experimentation I have spent on the driving range. Those who have had the rare opportunity to actually "play" a game with me would most likely argue that I did not actually play the game, so much as experiment my way around the golf course changing things from shot to shot, including the short game. This afforded me the opportunity to continue my investigation unhindered by the constant drive to lower my score. Admittedly, this is not how I would recommend any one else approach the game, but it was quite consistent with my personal objectives.

An added advantage is that my body configuration, segmental movement capacities, and neuromuscular functioning are all average and my problems in striking the ball effectively are basically similar to those of most other golfers. In other words, many of these suggested alterations (Options #1-6 in particular) have actually helped me, a less than gifted person, who has not uncommon problems in generating an effective swing.

An important point to consider is that most of the available literature, films, videos, and CD's, are put out by people who have experienced little difficulty in developing a highly successful, repeatable swing. They do a nice job at showing the viewer how to go about producing *their* swing, and cover many of the nuances involved in difficult shot making. However, the instructions are based on their movement capacities, not those of the average person. An example would be Hogan's Five Lessons which will be discussed in greater detail when Option #7 is presented.

Expectations During Stroke Modification

- That your ability to play the game will not improve while you are modifying your stroke pattern. In fact, during this learning process I suggest that you do not focus on scoring as much as on repatterning your swing. Should improvements in your swing emerge, the long-term benefits with regard to scoring will become evident as you integrate this new stroke into game situations.

- That success in modifying your swing will take time, effort, and perseverance.

- That learning will be enhanced by feedback from a golf pro, or someone with analytical skills.

- That video from frontal and lateral perspectives during lessons will enhance the learning process.

- That divots are significant , more important in technique alteration and experimentation stages than ball flight. It is unfortunate that so much attention is placed on ball flight after each shot, rather than the movement sequence. If the body mechanics are correct and the club path is right, the golfer is on the right track even though the ball may go off in the wrong direction. Such results could be due only to poor clubface alignment, a variable that can be fixed fairly easily.

The next section will contain suggestions for making changes to the full golf swing that might be of some benefit to the readers. Options #1-6 are intended for the average golfer with the classic tendency to move the club outside-in as it approaches ball contact. Option #7 is intended for those who strike the ball from an excessive inside-out path with the resulting inconsistency in ball travel that inevitably leads to erratic scoring. This alteration is not based on personal experience, since I have never possessed highly flexible thoracic vertebrae. Rather it is based on observing and working with a few overly flexible players.

Option # 1

This is the simplest of the alterations and is recommended for those who don't have the time, patience, or opportunity to make significant changes in the actual swing itself. It involves two adjustments, ball position, and club selection. Figure 60 illustrates the classic set-up for hitting with a driver.

This arrangement works well for those who can produce one of the successful club paths to contact. It is a set-up for failure for the average "horizontal hands at the transition" player. The less horizontal hand movement at the transition to the downswing, the better the result. This can be achieved by causing an earlier release pattern. One simply has to move the ball to the right in the stance, without changing the location of the rest of the body, as seen in Figure 61.

Figure 60

Figure 61

However, this alignment is aesthetically displeasing and results in the clubface aimed to the right of the target line. When the golfer squares the face it naturally decreases the loft. At the beginning of experimentation most people find that initiating the swing from this position is awkward. This is a normal reaction and due to years of conditioning. For most golfers using this alignment, a conventional driver with a loft of 9-11 degrees would not create the desired ball flight characteristics. They would find more comfort and greater success using a more lofted club such as a 3 or 5 wood.

I suggest that the player start the experiment with the ball teed one half inch above the ground in light rough, using a 3 wood. Position the ball 2-3 inches to the right of the left heel, and start hitting balls. Give this ball placement a reasonable number of strokes in order to determine if it is at the appropriate location. That is, to ensure that the club path is more in line with the intended direction of flight. If club path and ball flight remain typical for the player, move the ball to the right another inch and hit more balls. Continue to move the ball to the right at address until a more positive outcome (better club path as indicated by the grass imprint) results from each shot. If the path is good and the ball travels off to the right, simply take a "stronger" grip, that is pronate the left forearm/hand, and supinate the right. That adjustment should square the club at contact and lead to a straighter shot. It will take a short amount of time to adjust to this new position, and grip. Once you start to have better outcomes from your effort, however, the tendency will be to creep the ball more forward in your stance because of previous conditioning. This should be avoided for it will eventually lead back to the original problem.

This adjustment would have to be made for each club. One golfer might be most effective hitting tee shots using a 3 wood with the ball placed 2 inches to the right of center, with the wedges most effectively struck with the ball off the right toe. All of the adjustments are made according to each individual's needs and preferences, and some experimentation is necessary to find the most functional and repeatable swing.

The same immediate, and very informative feedback can be obtained by striking some irons from fluffy lies in the rough, without use of a tee. The path of the club up to and through contact is easy to determine, and if it is more in line with the intended target with the ball back in the stance, and yet the ball is not flying off in the right direction, then maintain the ball stance relationship, and alter the grip arrangement and pressure until the clubface is square and the ball flight desirable.

The above alteration may enable players to make better shots without having to change the actual swing components. Once the ball is in position, the proper club selected, and hands placed on the grip, the player can use their normal swing pattern and rhythm.

Professionals and low handicappers use this alteration when playing under wet conditions, or from a fairway bunker. They move the ball to the right in their stance at address, and then attempt to use their basic swing pattern. The ground reaction forces will be somewhat dissipated under these conditions, and they know from experience that their release mechanism, which is ingrained in their nervous system, will cause the release of the club at the same time in the flow of the swing, and that they will hit fat should they place the ball in the usual spot to the left. They can make this adjustment and still hit the ball straight at the target. This happens because the clubhead is basically on-line up to 12 inches prior to contact in the original position to the left at address. They, in effect, will be releasing the club earlier in their swing because they can't push forcefully enough against the softer ground substance to drive the body over the left foot early in the propulsive phase. This is similar to the objective in this first alteration, that is by placing the ball back in the stance, the golfer will be forced to release the striking mechanism (left arm pull and ulnar flexion) earlier, have less horizontal hand movement in the early striking phase, and as a result cause a more in-line path of the club to the point of collision.

Option # 2

This is next in the order of difficulty because it involves a conscious change in the delivery of the propulsive phase of the stroke. Should the golfer find that Option #1 does not completely bring about an in-line club path, I suggest an additional factor be added to the ball position and club selection previously discussed. It follows the same principle, that is, to limit the horizontal movement of the hands at transition to downswing. It is simple in concept, but takes time to master.

Players should follow their usual steps in the preparatory phase of the swing, and once the transition position is reached should initiate the downswing by consciously pulling the left arm down first. The left scapula is fully abducted and the left shoulder joint in full horizontal adduction at the transition, and contraction of the prime movers of this region at this time will cause the hands to move more vertically than horizontally and the resulting club path should be more in-line and ball contact more desirable (Figure 62).

Figure 62

In the beginning, this is difficult to perform, because the player has loaded the right side, and is primed to rotate the pelvis and take with it all the upper segments of the body. By contracting the shoulder girdle and shoulder joint muscles ahead of their natural sequence, the body contribution is decreased, there is a loss of momentum from the lower segments, but the primary objective of proper club path, with reasonably good velocity, will be achieved. *Option #2 must be performed without a noticeable shift in the body's center of gravity. The right leg must be fixed so that little or no backward displacement occurs (see Chapter IV).*

With this modification, the player, when viewing the video, will see that the pelvis has neither rotated nor moved to the left as much when the club has made contact with the ball. The resulting shots, once the player has become accustomed to using this adaptation, will be more accurate and reliable, in spite of the fact that the lower segments of the body are not contributing to their full potential.

With this swing modification, there will be a tendency for less total momentum to be involved, and as a result the follow-through will see less of the total body mass over the left foot. This, to be sure, compromises our natural tendency to use all of our body parts to the fullest, in order to achieve greater clubhead velocity at contact. However, for some, this adaptation might prove helpful in gaining control over clubhead path to ball contact, cut down on the variability of the outcomes, and as a result, reduce scores.

For some, a combination of options #1 & #2 might prove effective. For others a single modification might help square-up the contact and lead to more predictable shot making.

Although I've emphasized the major adjustments for options #1 & #2, other factors such as placement of the feet (both in terms of spacing and alignment), and hands (a myriad of grip options), can also be experimented with in order for the whole swing to work.

In addition, those who wish to improve shot making without major swing alterations can experiment with speeding up the entire swing from initiation of the backswing to follow through. It has been my experience that by making a commitment to a very fast backswing (particularly the first 90 degrees) that a successful unweighting will occur, and a sufficient though not complete torqueing of the upper body will also take place (Figure 63). The bending of the shaft indicates a very fast movement of the hands with a firm grip at the very start of the backswing. The immediate reversal and commitment to the striking phase will prevent overloading of the outward rotators of the right hip joint and result in a more vertical than horizontal movement of the hands at the initiation of the downswing.

Consider the number of very competent players at your own club who have what are obviously very fast swings. Visualize many of the players on the three tours and you will also come up with a large number of great professional players who also have very fast swings. There is a very good reason for this approach, and I venture the opinion that when asked to slow down their swings, these players would completely lose their ability to pull off the shots that they can easily make on a routine basis. "Low and slow" to initiate the backswing can be just the right set-up for failure for many. Lacking thoracic and shoulder flexibility, a 'low and slow' first 90 degrees will force the player to pull back with the right hand by adducting the right scapula and horizontally abducting the right shoulder joint, in order to get the club to horizontal, which for some reason is thought by most teachers to be the ideal. The drawing back motion using the right arm and hand will bring about the locking mechanism and result in the usual problems.

Figure 63

The process of experimenting with Options #1 and #2, by changing the tempo to a faster rhythm, or by a combination of these may help the player to gain knowledge of their body, and ultimately come to an improved swing without having to completely change their basic patterns of movement.

Option # 3

This involves major changes in concept, feel, and movement patterns. Everything you have read, heard, or been taught about the golf swing is inconsistent with what follows. However, you are not unfamiliar with this approach, for you see it demonstrated virtually every time you turn on one of the professional tournaments. The problem is that the TV analysts, most golf teachers, and "purists", refer to the swings I am about to present as unique to the individuals, and not to be copied or in any way emulated by those either beginning to learn the game or those trying to reshape their swings. These swings look funny, they vary from the traditional model, and apparently should only be used by special individuals. I'm not so sure.

It is obvious from the performance of players like Jim Furyk, Lee Trevino, and Allen Doyle that they meet the required ball striking characteristics with great consistency. They, like many others, accomplish this very demanding task with complete swing patterns that are uniquely their own. As previously presented, the greatest variations in the golf swing appear during the preparation and transition phases rather than in the striking/propulsive phase. It is this component (prepatory) that will be emphasized, in the hopes that, should the golfer attempt this approach, it will be understood that this is a very difficult approach to master, particularly when it goes against everything you've thought or done up to this point in your golfing experience.

There are four essential elements to this swing approach. Each person, as one would expect, will perform these with their own particular rhythm, range of motion, and style.

Element # 1 — From the address position, the clubhead is moved outside the direct line of the intended flight of the ball. This occurs either at the very outset, or after the club has been moved directly backwards for a foot or two. This creates the desired momentum shift to the right side (Figure 64 and 65).

Element # 2 — As the arms continue to rise beyond the horizontal, there is still no contact between the left upper arm and the chest (Figure 66).

The reason for this is that the motion is performed at the shoulder girdle and shoulder joints when the club is moved to the outside. When it is moved directly back and then to the inside as is traditional, contact is made at different times for each individual depending on the conformation of the chest and arms. Those with the appropriate ectomorphic (lean) body type experience little difficulty with the traditional backswing move.

Figure 64

Figure 65

Figure 66

Figure 67

Figure 68

Most of us however, make contact early, and cause the thorax (chest) to become engaged prematurely in the preparation phase. Because there is no early left arm contact with the chest in this particular swing, and a good portion of the drawback occurrs in the shoulders, there's little thoracic rotation early on, and therefore little transfer to the lower body. In other words, the pelvis, although now part of the swing, is not caused to rotate at both hip joints to the same extent as with the normal preparatory movements.

Element # 3 — The unweighting of the left side is completed before the left arm is brought toward the sternum (horizontal adduction of the left shoulder joint). While this is occurring, the lower body will have already begun to move to the left and if some pelvic rotation to the right has also occurred, it will begin to rotate to the left as well (Figure 67).

Element # 4 - Because the left arm contact has been delayed and less pelvic rotation has occurred, the hands, as they start the propulsive phase, will not be forced horizontally, but will follow a more vertical path (Figure 68).

The rest of the propulsive phase should follow the same sequential segmental pattern as previously discussed: trunk, shoulder girdle, shoulder joints, hands, club. With swings similar to Jim Furyk's, the right elbow may actually move behind the body during the downswing.

It is difficult to put a timeframe on the learning process for this swing. I suggest that for the first few lessons, each shot should be teed at a comfortable height. Try not to become concerned with maximum distances at first. If you can obtain a direct path to contact, it will only be a matter of time before you learn to control the clubface angle and to determine your position from the ball in order to hit the sweet spot.

Option #4

It can be seen that traditional approaches to set-up, take-away, transition and downswing have not worked effectively for the average person. The low and slow backswing coupled with the parallel shaft position at the top, literally forces us to place body parts in such a way that a vigorous and ballistic swing will inevitably lead to an undesirable result. Another way to avoid this is to set in motion a series of movements that preclude this from happening. This option involves a wider stance than normal, a very rapid and limited preparatory move, and a brief but effective unweighting and reweighting of the left side. Figure 69 shows the set-up, Figure 70, the initiation of the rapid back swing, Figure 71, temporary unweighting, Figure 72, the transition to down swing. The swing is completed in approximately half a second. The best example of this approach is Allen Doyle, one of the most consistent and successful players on the Champions tour. Another famous player, considered by many to be the greatest ballstriker of all time, Moe Norman, also approaches the swing with these characteristics.

Figure 69

Figure 70

Figure 71

Figure 72

Why does this work? The necessary movements are performed without premature contact of the left arm to the chest. The hands are never high enough to overly elevate the left scapula. The delivery is accomplished with such speed that the hands never have a chance to drift horizontally prior to club release. This procedure does require the capacity to accelerate the clubhead over a short distance, and may be difficult for some to adjust to. Radial flexion during the latter stage of the backswing/transition and the ulnar flexion that occurs immediately thereafter, require reasonably strong forearms and hands. Many without the requisite anatomical features will find this both difficult and uncomfortable. It will not appeal to anyone with weak hands and forearms.

Option #5

Now, conjure up a mental image of players such as Ken Perry, Tom Lehman, Johnny Miller, * and Lee Janzen. Although their swings differ in timing and loci of movements, they not only share the essential characteristics of good ball striking, but also share an important movement in the initiation of the downswing. All four, and many others on tour, appear to begin the propulsive phase with a noticeable downward movement of the body. However, in reality, it is a combined downward/forward movement that takes place. A rapid release of the tension in the right quadriceps and hamstrings at the transition results in a downward motion of the body. This is followed by a strong contraction of these muscles together with the right hip abductors. These contractions move the center of gravity toward the left foot. As this is happening, the player contracts the left internal oblique muscle and right external oblique muscle to cause both a rotation and flexion of the trunk. These combined movements cause the trunk and head to dip, and more importantly causes the hands to move downward as propulsion is initiated. This pattern of movement accomplishes three things. It speeds the desired rotation by combining with the left back muscles (iliocostalis lumborum, latissimus dorsi), it diminishes the outward rotation of the right hip joint by lessening the stretch/contract effect of the right hamstrings, and, as mentioned, directs the hands more vertically at the beginning of the downswing. Figures 73-76 illustrate this maneuver.

One of the characteristics of this approach is that it generally leads to a more downward-forward clubhead approach to the ball, which leads to a significant divot on iron shots from the fairway. The forward body movement of this swing is crucial, for without it, the body will stay either on the right leg or centered between both legs, and the club will be directed vertically into the ground, and result in a less than desirable vibration of the club in the player's hands, and of course a poor shot. I found it easier to start learning this method with a fairway wood, the ball teed an inch or two off the ground, and placed three-four inches further away from my normal club set-up. This will allow any possible errors in the beginning of the experiment to take place without causing injury.

At the start I suggest a less than all-out swing. As one becomes accustomed to this striking method, a gradual increase in speed of movement, together with an adjustment of the ball placement will make learning easier and more efficient.

Option #6

As helpful as Option #4 will be for selected individuals with the appropriate upper limb capacities, and Options #3 and #5 for those with the time and neuromuscular skills to learn them, these may not suit a large segment of the golfing population. This, the last option suggested for the average player, just might be the easiest to learn, and result in the best opportunity for improvement for the greatest number of golfers. The irony is that a number of successful players throughout the history of golf have used this approach, but it has been

* An excellent article on this swing technique was written by Johnny Miller and can be found in *Golf Digest*, June 1995.

Figure 73

Figure 74

Figure 75

Figure 76

downgraded so often by many of the teaching gurus both in print and on TV, that people have simply not chosen to even try it.* Perhaps the best exponent of this stroking technique was a man many have opined to be the greatest player of all time, Bobby Jones. A great many readers will have seen his series on the Golf Channel, and perhaps have noticed just how he went about striking the ball. Some of the movements and positions I will discuss are now considered major flaws for serious golfers who aspire to championship play. I maintain that his approach is very well suited to most average golfers, because it is clear that he himself did not possess the high degree of thoracic rotation exhibited by many of the golfers today. How did he take what appears to be an average body and turn out long and accurate, repeatable shots? Let's examine his technique.

Figures 77-78 illustrates the Option #6 set-up. I recommend that the reader start with feet turned out (45 degrees) and the heels at least one foot apart, with *very* slight angulation of the trunk, the arms and forearms (if possible) in contact with the front of the body and the club grounded with light downward pressure applied. If more rotation is necessary, greater outward rotation of the right hip joint will turn the right foot to a more open stance, and permit greater range of motion.

There is an added benefit resulting from outwardly rotating the right hip joint, that being the effect it has on the pelvis when the player hyperextends that knee during the backswing. It forces the pelvis to move directly backward which prevents the undesired sliding of the pelvis over the right foot.

Figure 77

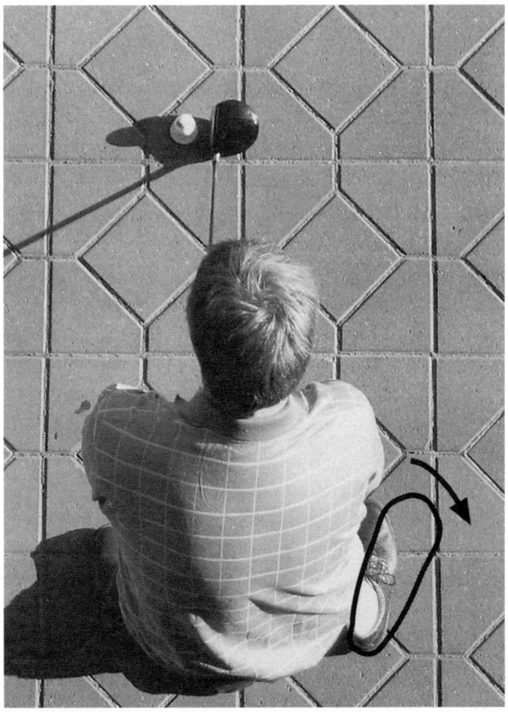

Figure 78

* An excellent article on this swing technique was written by Don Wade, and can be found in *Golf World Annual*, February 1983.

From this position the swing is started not by a rearward movement of the club, but by a forward rotation of the pelvis and right thigh as seen in Figure 79. During this action the light pressure on the clubhead prevents its movement. This unweights the right side and allows the player to initiate a vigorous push with the left leg driving the lower body into a rapid rotation in the opposite direction initiating the backswing. This push with the left leg is followed immediately by extension of the right hip and knee which leads to the knee being hyperextended (Figures 80 and 81). It is important to note that extending the right hip and knee from an outwardly rotated starting position (Figures 92 and 93) will cause the pelvis to rotate directly to the rear, which will result in the right leg angled forward preventing any drift in the center of gravity. It leads to loading the right, unweighting the left, with virtually no shift in the center of gravity. The clubhead remains on the ground until it is pulled backward and inward by the hands which have been pulled by the body. The dynamic movement of the lower body precedes the trunk, arms and club and arrives at the transition well before the arms and club have reached their final backward position. If done properly, the lower body initiates its downswing motion while the hands are still moving backward.

Figure 79

Figure 80

Figure 81

Initiating the swing with a dynamic rotation of the lower body first, should result in hyperextension of the right knee and a movement of the club directly to the inside of the target line as shown in Figures 80 and 81.

All of these movements will result in a desired unweighting of the left side, an early rotation of the lower body to initiate the downswing, a delayed effect on the hands, and a more vertical movement of the hands at the transition to downswing.

However, in order for the hands to complete the backswing the player must abduct both shoulder joints, flex the right elbow, and radially flex both wrists. Figures 82 and 83 show the end position resulting from this combination of movements. The club should be *at or past* the horizontal and beyond the commonly taught parallel alignment to the target line. Although this is generally not recommended, there is a very important positive effect.

Figure 82

Figure 83

By placing the hands and club further behind the body, any horizontal movement of the hands that starts the downswing will cause their position to be very much closer to the "ideal" spot in space when they start their downward motion toward the ball. This can be seen in Figures 84-89 where the hands have moved vertically when in line with the body, much like the approach of the more flexible individuals who use the commonly taught approach to ball striking. The timing of the vertical movement comes earlier relative to the instant of ball strike, and permits the club to approach from a more direct line to the ball, avoiding the dreaded outside-in path.

Figure 84

Figure 85

Figure 86

Referring to the films of Bobby Jones, the reader can see that as he moves from shorter to longer clubs, he amplifies this crossing over. This gives him the opportunity to 'spin out' at the transition to downswing at the top, and not cause the hands to drift horizontally in front of his body before their release.

Figure 87

Figure 88

Figure 89

This swing is easier to perform because one does not have to separate the action of the thorax from that of the pelvis during the preparatory phase. The entire trunk moves as a unit, with concomitant motion at both feet, knees, and hip joints. As a result there is less tension, and less strain on the muscles and joints of the body, particularly the lower back. It is my belief that this swing will be very comfortable for many readers, that they will perform this approach with greater ease and with more success. The more "inside" the takeaway, the more flexible the hip joints, the more crossover of the club at the top, and the deeper the hands move behind the body at the top of the backswing, the more distance they can move horizontally before they reach a position where the hands are in line with the lateral side of the body, just where the vertical move should begin. In other words it gives the player a greater margin for error, more horizontal hand movement without having the hands or club move to the outside in front of the body causing the outside-in swing.

Although flexible golfers such as John Daly place the club well beyond the horizontal and parallel, this is done as part of a natural evolution of their particular swing, and is not required to eliminate the horizontal spin out maneuver that the rest of us naturally perform. In fact his thoracic/pelvic flexibility appears to be quite substantial, and his hands move nearly vertically throughout the downswing. If he were to set his hands lower and more behind his body, he would hook the ball, or failing to close the face of the club, push the shot severely to the right.

The very idea that positioning the club in that manner (beyond horizontal, crossed-over line) will automatically lead to poor results, is simply wrong. Everything depends on where the hands are and their path of movement when they are accelerated. The hands can, in fact, move horizontally to a considerable degree provided they are lateral to the right side of the body when they are finally moved vertically and accelerated.

A shorter version of this swing works quite well, and is recommended for older players and those with shoulder injuries, such as impingement syndromes (rotator cuff, long head of biceps). Figures 90-98 show Option #6 with the club not reaching parallel.

Figure 90

Figure 91

Figure 92

Figure 93

Figure 94

Figure 95

Figure 96

Figure 97

Figure 98

Option # 7

This modification, unlike the previous six, is not targeted for the greatest percentage of golfers, but is recommended for those with too much of a good thing. These individuals have an excessive amount of movement capability in the upper body components and as a result have the problem of moving their hands too vertically (sometimes downward and backward) during the transition and downswing (Figure 99). The club is released toward the collision from an extreme inside-out path, and the resulting shots often end up in less than desirable locations. These are the individuals at your club who can start a drive out over the right side rough and draw (hook) the ball into the left side rough. This often leads to long hitting, but many times less than commensurate scoring.

This is, in my opinion, an easier problem to fix. The suggestions may seem familiar to those who have read Ben Hogan's wonderfully insightful *The Modern Fundamentals of Golf*, and there is a good reason for this. Every one of his recommendations is helpful to the over-flexible, excessive draw, reasonably long hitting golfer who can't score to his/her potential.

Figure 99

Element # 1— By "playing from the insides of your thighs" (isometrically contracting the adductors of both hip joints), one primarily restricts lateral movement, and to a lesser extent rotary movements of the pelvis (Figures 100-103). This reduces the degrees of freedom during the preparation, and serves as a significant landmark position that signifies the end-point of motion for the lower body segment.

Some may use the term 'anchor', as it connotes a repeatable locking mechanism for easy reproduction of the same swing pattern. Those who have great flexibility, but do not have a technique to know where their body parts are in space and time, are always trying to guess where and when to deliver each segmental contribution. When they are hot, they can score well, when not, they tend to spray, and the scores go up. This is seen quite often on the tours, where an individual's scores may vary as much as ten or twelve strokes from day to day, and this variation may be traced to a significant drop in number of fairways landed and number of greens in regulation.

Figure 100

Figure 101

Figure 102

Figure 103

Element # 2 — Another way to center and restrict pelvic motion is to outwardly rotate the left hip joint (Figure 104). This opens the stance by placing the left foot at less than a perpendicular angle to the intended line of flight. The more outward rotation, the tighter the pubo-femoral ligament, and the greater the restriction of motion.

Element # 3 — The last adjustment of Hogan's to discuss is the use of the hands. His description and illustrations lead us to believe that he accomplished left wrist flexion during the final stages of the downswing. In reality, his left wrist is very near a neutral position at contact, and it comes about as a result of previous contractions, not due to any conscious motion on his part. (Hogan used the term 'supination' to describe this wrist position. However, since supination/pronation occur in the radio-ulnar joints his description was inaccurate on both counts.)

Element # 4 — In addition to the Hogan recommendations, I might add that this problem may also benefit from a more upright preparatory phase (Figure 105).

Figure 104

Figure 105

When the hands are placed too much to the rear at transition, and are pulled too vertically to start the downswing, they must travel horizontally later in the striking phase, and by doing so cause the clubhead to approach from too severe an inside path. It also may cause a very late release of the hands, not permitting the clubhead enough time to stabilize before impact.

Again, the vast majority of golfers with limited thoracic rotation would not do well should they attempt all of these adjustments particularly from a position of significant forward trunk angulation. It must be remembered that Hogan shaped his swing to eliminate a strong hook. He had great insights into the solution to his problem. Option #7 will work for a very select group of golfers, those who have to deal with having too much of a good thing.

Other Possibilities

This section is for those who have the time and inclination to venture further into many of the kinesiological possibilities inherent in the full golf swing. The following is not meant to be a complete coverage, but merely a few of the more interesting experiments.

Often analysts point out that right hand tension too early in the downswing is the cause of the casting movement leading to the outside-in path to contact. It has been my experience that either hand can be the source of the problem. Both right hand tension and its very placement on the grip can produce undesired forces on the club. However, I have found that it is left hand tension that solidifies the hands to the club and the left arm to the body. This results in transferring the spin out of the body to the hands and club. There are a number of possible alterations to left hand functioning that can be experimented with.

Hands #1 – A simple adjustment is to extend the little finger and completely eliminate it from the left hand grip (Figure 106).

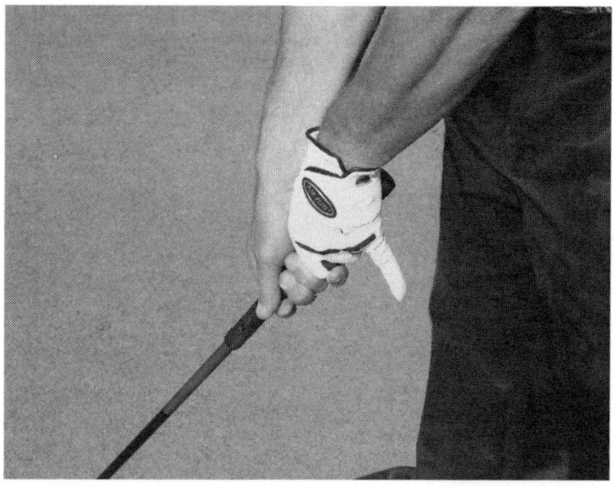

Figure 106

Figure 107

Figure 108

Hands #2 – Another alteration is to release three fingers (middle, ring, and little) of the left hand prior to the transition. This will accomplish three things. It will dramatically soften the tension transmitted to the handle. It will decrease the lockout tension when the right hand and arm pull on the club to get the low and slow backswing to the top. (You will not feel the body move to the right and out of position at the top.) It will increase the tendency for a delay in hand action (Figure 107). Completing the propulsive phase without regripping will change your release pattern considerably, so any attempt to strike the ball without a regrip will take time to master. One can still contribute effort to the swing with the left arm and transfer the pull through the index and thumb which are still on the handle. However this is not an easy change to make. Regripping at the very end of the transition and beginning of the downswing is, of course, a difficult maneuver (Figure 108). If one can time this properly, it will result in a more vertical path of the hands with an increase of power to the stroke. However, since this is a very tricky alteration, I recommend initial attempts be made without a ball. Once you are convinced that a reasonable timing has been developed, slowly start to hit teed balls with a short iron, and if it proves promising, move to longer clubs.

Hands #3 — Another possibility is to flex the ring and little finger of the left hand before gripping the club (Figures 109-111). This will accomplish the same type of effect as Hands #2, but might prove uncomfortable for many who try it. If it works for you but is uncomfortable, try placing pads on the last digits of the two flexed fingers where they make contact with the handle.

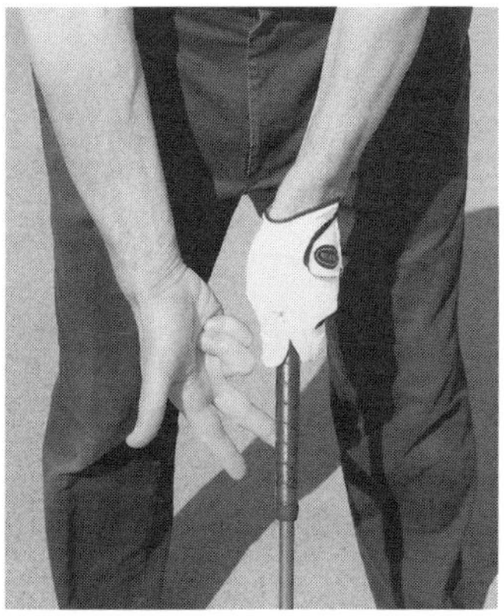
Figure 109

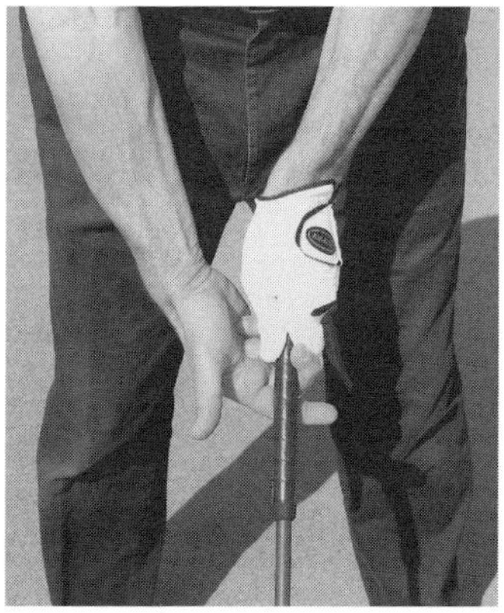
Figure 110

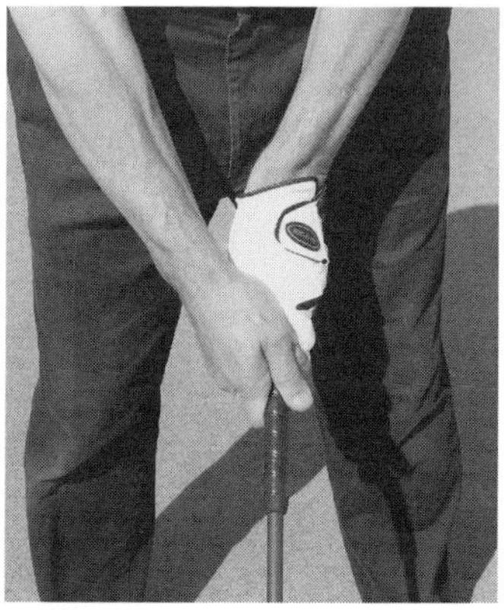
Figure 111

Hands #4 — The fourth recommendation is to remove the left thumb from the handle completely (Figure 112). For many this will soften the handle connection and decrease the casting effect. I have found this to be less effective than the above suggestions. However, the whole purpose of this book is to have the reader experiment to find the best personal approach to ball striking.

Any right hand grip will cause a dramatic casting effect for the average slicer as long as the left hand remains firm. An open right hand in its traditional position at the top and maintained throughout the acceleration of the club, will exert as much undesired outward force as a tight right hand grip. In fact, because it will lose its opportunity to pull the clubhead back during the latter stages of acceleration, it will result in a greater problem than the tight grip throughout (Figure 113).

Hands #5 — Placing the handle between the index and middle finger of the right hand (Figure 114) alters the force transference during club acceleration and might help some golfers with the transition to downswing and path to contact. I found it useful but painful, even after placing padding at the base between the two fingers. Others have found it helpful and not the least injurious. I would recommend caution with this approach. Start swinging slowly without striking any balls. Gradually increase the intensity of effort and determine if the movements themselves produce discomfort. If not, tee up some balls and start swinging slowly with a short iron. One member at Oakfield (single digit handicap) has played with it for a couple of years and is comfortable with it.

Figure 112

Figure 113

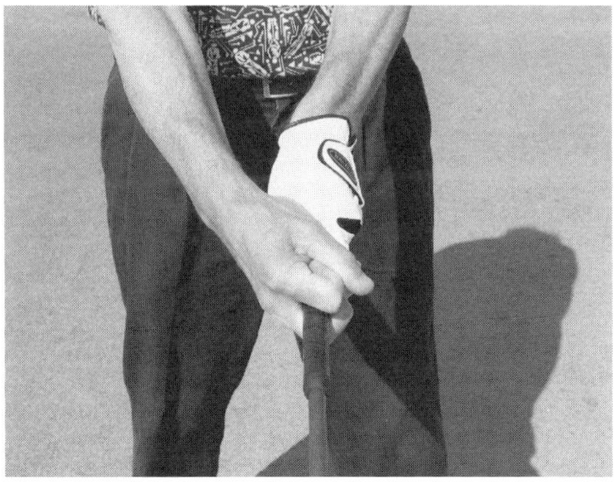

Figure 114

Figure 115

Figure 116

Hands #6 – Figure 115 shows a traditional grip with the shaft and forearms forming a "Y" at the address position. This tends to square up the shoulders, and tends to cause hyperextension of both wrists at the top of the swing, along with radial flexion. This will often lead to a more horizontal release of the clubhead.

Figure 116 shows a more supinated left forearm with the shaft and left arm in a nearly straight line. This results in slight flexion of the left wrist and slight hyperextension in the right wrist. This often helps with a better club position at the top and more vertical movement to initiate the downswing.

Feet #1 — The feet are obviously of great importance. They support the body, apply all the forces generated by the body to the ground, and influence the positions and movement excursions of much of the body.

The address position of the feet with both hips outwardly rotated and the trunk erect encourages a more singular unit movement of the entire body during the backswing, as explained in Option #6. This is more of a three-segment swing used by Bobby Jones and on the ladies' tour, Laura Davies. Wide spacing of the feet, a square right foot, together with forward trunk angulation encourages the separation of thorax from pelvis and the use of a four-segment swing demonstrated by many of today's professionals and top amateurs.

Figure 117

Figure 118

A wide stance (Figure 117) works best with a faster backswing and therefore a rapid complete swing in order for the player to take advantage of the gravitational acceleration of the body during the brief non-support (unweighted) period. A wide stance, slow swing can be accomplished by only a few, very flexible individuals.

Feet #2 — Opening the stance by placing the left foot at an angle to the perpendicular (outward rotation of the left hip joint) tends to restrict pelvic motion during the backswing, as previously discussed. Rotating the right foot away from the perpendicular (outward rotation of the right hip joint) tends to encourage lower body rotation during the preparatory phase. The latter may be of benefit to the average player, the former to the lower handicappers. By inwardly rotating the left hip joint, the average player will find it easier to encourage an unweighting of the left side (Figure 118). During the downswing a pivot will be necessary to assume a position of outward rotation to accept the body weight comfortably at the end of the swing.

Chest #1 — This part of the anatomy is often overlooked when instruction is given, yet the degree of inhalation, particularly for a person with a large vital capacity, can have a significant effect. I've found that full inhalation and an isometric holding of the chest during the swing tends to separate the arms unnecessarily, causes early left arm contact, and generally interferes with the swing. I recommend experimentation with different levels of inspiration/expiration before holding a given position, and observing the effects on the outcome.

Head/Neck #1 — Assuming a normal slightly flexed head/neck position during the swing is most comfortable for the majority of golfers. However, with some great golfers this position allows the left shoulder (acromion) to move beneath the chin during the backswing, yet with others who turn less, the upper humerus stops beneath the chin. In either case the good ball strikers start the hands into the downswing in one of the acceptable patterns. Most of us don't.

Readers should keep in mind that at the top of the swing, they must make a conscious effort to keep the head and neck facing the ball. This requires a fairly strong contraction of the right sterno-mastoid muscle and the left splenius capitus. It is similar to the position illustrated in Figure 119, where the player has simply rotated his head to face the target. With this in mind, readers might experiment with starting the backswing while facing the target. It will be noticed that at the top of the swing they are facing directly at the ball (Figure 120), and they will have arrived there with little strain. Some might find this off-putting, but others may find it quite comfortable. Starting this at a slower pace would make the process that much easier.

Figure 119

Figure 120

Head/Neck #2 — The considerable effect of head and neck position *and tension* on hand path can be seen when one attempts to strike a ball with the head rotated fully to the right during the entire swing. In fact it took a very long time for me to actually make contact in this position because the club always approached from further inside the line than I anticipated. Releasing tension in the head and neck musculature that would normally lock the entire body together at the top of the average player's swing, encourages a more vertical descent of the hands at the transition and early downswing. This can be seen in Figures 121-124. Unfortunately, until someone makes glasses that will allow a player to 'see' and get accustomed to this, I doubt that many will experiment with it for too long.

Figure 121

Figure 122

Figure 123

Figure 124

CHAPTER IV

Clarification of Concepts

Earlier, I mentioned a number of ideas that would require further elaboration. There are concerns related to the preparatory phase, the relationship of the center of mass to the right leg/foot, and the hand-foot concept and how it applies to the full golf swing.

Preparatory Phase

The approach employed by many instructors when teaching the take-away, tends to emphasize a low and slow beginning movement. For those with the upper body flexibility and a nervous system conducive to this speed of movement, it works just fine. For the golfer with average or less than average movement capabilities, this often proves to be the first mistake in the swing.

With more than normal range of motion in the facet joints of the thoracic spine, and tissue elasticity in the back musculature, even a slow movement backward will create enough momentum to keep torqueing the pliant individual, and will also create a significant unweighting of the left foot. It is interesting to note that many of these golfers do not lift the left heel from the ground, and yet achieve a true loading of the right lower quadrant of the body. How much the left heel moves depends on a few factors, not the least of which is upper body flexibility. How much others lift it, would depend on the width of stance, speed of the initial take-away, and body tissue elasticity.

There is no single position or elevation that can apply to all. However, for the less flexible, it is my belief that this is an essential element in the swing, for if solid ground contact is maintained with the left foot, both the inward rotators and extensors of the left hip are loaded and when contracted will contribute to the pelvic spin out. This causes the hands to move horizontally at transition and the initiation of the crucial mistake made by most golfers. The spin out can happen even if the left heel is lifted, provided there is substantial body weight still over this foot. A fast loading of the right and unloading of the left at transition time will correct this problem. Close observation of Jack Nicklaus will reveal that his left heel is moving upwardly at transition time. Control of his left leg/foot is a significant part of his successful swing.

A rapid first half of the backswing, may often be more effective for the average golfer, as long as this motion creates enough momentum to unweight the left foot, sufficiently torque the upper body (without excessive pelvic rotation), eliminate the need to pull back with the right shoulder girdle muscles (causing the dreaded lock-up), and not create any tension in the left hand. If a softness at transition, or a "floating to the top feeling" is experienced, this will set up an effective transition, and a powerful striking motion, with one of the better club paths to contact.

In order to experience this effect, it might prove helpful to go to extremes by moving as slowly as possible for the entire backswing and notice on the video how you must adjust your body movements in order to get the club at or near a horizontal position. Then initiate your backswing at a fast tempo and observe whether or not the patterns change dramatically. I suggest that you do this without attempting to hit a ball at first, then after you've observed the differences, try hitting balls from a tee. This process will be enhanced if you do not ground the club. With no resistance to the first movement that initiates the backswing, the club will accelerate quickly and develop greater momentum at an earlier stage in this preparatory phase. Remember, there are many great players on tour who have abbreviated backswings combined with a very fast tempo. This means that they explode from the very beginning, float and transfer the weight back to the left side quickly to begin the striking phase.

Center of Mass and the Right Leg/Foot

This factor is critical to both the proper sequential segmental movement pattern and the tempo with which this pattern is carried out. With a full golf swing, the narrower the stance, the more the golfer has to rely on rotational movements, both in the preparatory and propulsive phases. This will significantly affect the possible contribution of the lower body. The center of mass (center of gravity) of the body will travel very small distances with a narrow stance and will usually require a slower tempo for swing completion. The slowness of tempo becomes more apparent as the golfer shifts the center of mass more directly over the right foot. With a wider stance, as previously discussed, the speed of both the unweighting during the backswing, and the reweighting to begin the striking phase, must occur at a fast tempo in order to accomplish all of the desired objectives. The reader, of course, is familiar with this type of approach as there are many examples on the professional tours. It would be interesting to determine how effective these fast tempo players would be, should they try to slow the tempo or rhythm of their swing patterns. I believe that they would have great difficulty adjusting, and their accurate, repeatable swings would not be possible.

The rhythm has to be faster for most wide-stance players because of the gravitational forces acting on the center of mass as soon as the momentum shifts to the right leg/foot. The left foot registers little force during this unweighting, yet the center of mass is still a considerable distance from the right foot (Figure 125). *At this point in time the body weight is loaded onto the right leg/foot, not shifted over the right leg/foot. Most great ball strikers do not shift the center of mass over the right side.* Essentially the body is hanging in space, because the center of mass is largely unsupported by the left leg and gravity will cause a falling tendency toward the ground. This, together with the abduction of the right hip and the combined extension of the right hip and knee, will drive the body forward, and for some slightly downward. In this short time period, the fast tempo golfer must make the transition and begin the striking phase.

This section seems like the best place to introduce another misconception that has been bandied about as a result of a recent replication of a study that was originally presented many years ago. It consisted of a golfer standing with both feet on separate spring scales, and the accompanying film showed that a large percentage of the golfer's body weight was on the right foot at contact.* This, to me, represents a misapplication of the scientific approach, as the authors used an inappropriate measuring technique (unidimensional with a time lag), and then drew conclusions that are simply inaccurate. Studies at Dalhousie University comparing a spring scale to a force platform clearly show that, for an excellent ball striker, the gravitational forces are almost entirely on the left foot immediately prior to contact on a full golf drive (when measured on a force platform). Unfortunately, many teachers and players have been attempting to duplicate the results of the spring scale study and maintain body weight over the right side through contact. This, of course, is not desirable, and will only serve to make what is already a difficult skill that much more confusing. Even using Option #2, golfers should not consciously attempt to maintain their weight over the rear foot.

Figure 125

* *Golf Digest*, April 1989.

There are several ways to ensure the proper relationship between the body's center of mass and the right foot. The first two have already been discussed, the width of stance, and the backswing speed. These factors have to be experimented with in order for each person to find the right combination of placement and tempo. If a successful combination cannot be found, and there still appears to be too much shift of the lower body over the right foot, or excessive pelvic rotation, then experimentation with one of the following might prove helpful.

Figure 126

Adduction of the right hip joint prior to the initiation of the backswing (Figure 126), results in the right knee moving toward the left knee.

Once this position is reached the golfer holds it for part or all of the preparatory phase. The amount of force exerted during the isometric contraction and the length of the effort is an individual matter, and will depend on the speed of the initial phase of the drawback (the momentum created), and the overall length of the preparatory phase. It should serve the purpose of lessening the movement of the pelvis and center of mass to the right without eliminating the unweighting of the left side. To do this effectively, the average golfer might have to speedup the beginning of the backswing.

Although I cautioned about using the Hogan adaptations for most average golfers, another possibility is to try his maneuver of adducting both hip joints simultaneously before beginning the backswing and holding the position for part or all of the preparatory phase (Figures 127 and 128).

Figure 127

Figure 128

Again, this will feel very different, but will accomplish the same goals as the single hip adduction mentioned above. In fact, it will cause even more of a centering of the lower body. It will not suit everyone. In fact, it may prove to be quite uncomfortable for some, particularly older and less flexible players. This approach will have to be used with a faster initial portion of the backswing in order for the unweighting-reweighting of the left side to occur properly. Interestingly, I played my best front nine at Oakfield (2 under) using this swing adaptation, but changed strokes for the back nine because of discomfort in my low back. It served the purpose of centering my swing and made for consistent contacts and good ball flights, but I found it uncomfortable to perform. Of course, hitting three buckets of balls prior to the round may also have contributed to the discomfort.

Some might find a more subtle modification to be helpful in maintaining a proper positioning of the pelvis and lower body during the preparatory phase. It involves an unusual set of isometric contractions that are performed at address and held through most or all of the preparatory phase. Figures 129 and 130 show a close up of the right foot with both a normal stance and with the modification suggested.

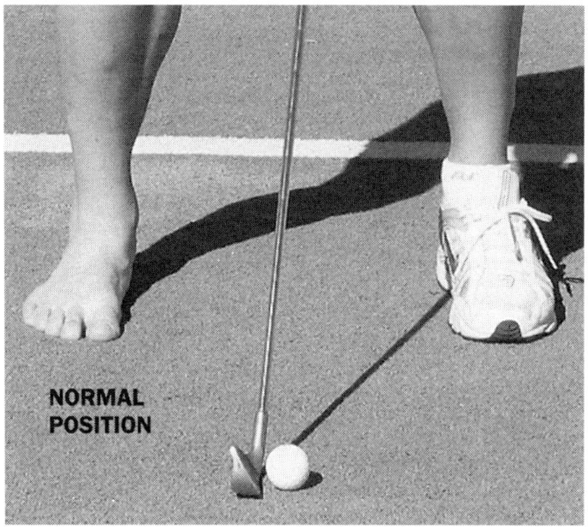

Figure 129

Figure 130

This change is accomplished by first concentrically contracting three of the anterior muscles of the lower leg (extensor hallicus longus, extensor digitorum longus, peroneus tertius) then holding this position via an isometric contraction of these muscles for the duration of the swing. Although it will feel strange at first, the tension created by hyperextending the toes will prevent the foot from inverting (rolling over) during the backswing. And this will tend to center the center of mass, keeping it to the inside of the right foot. The contraction isolates the ankle and foot, particularly the subtalar and intertarsal joints, reducing the possibility of the body rolling over the right foot which places the weight on the outer or lateral border of the foot. The overall effect is to keep the centering without eliminating the unweighting-reweighting sequence.

One of the effects is that it may feel as if there is more weight concentrated on the right heel, and that pushing off from the right foot is not as easy as one's usual swing. However, it may have an overall beneficial effect by both centering the player and lessening the horizontal hand movement at transition. This, as with all swing changes will feel awkward at first, but may in the long run work for some.

The final centering procedure has already been covered in Option #6. Hyperextending the right knee during the backswing not only loads the joint giving the same anchor, its momentum forces the pelvis to rotate backwards, preventing the unwanted sliding movement over the right foot. Another approach is to preset this position before initiating the backswing (Figure 131).

Figure 131 Hyperextended Right Knee

Although this book is intended primarily for the average player, it is my belief that many low handicappers and pros, even the touring pros, could benefit from applying one of these centering procedures. It is obvious from the dispersion of their drives and the inconsistencies in their approach shots to the greens, that many players do not have a stopping point in their swing. By this, I mean a mechanism that ensures the exact same position has been achieved in the preparatory sequence with regard to the position of the player's center of mass and each of the components that contribute to that center. In other words, they are guessing as to where they are in space, and the timing has to be perfect for them to execute the shot as intended. One of the keys to this is to focus on the right knee of a player as a full swing is executed. If it moves to the right one inch for one swing and then more or less for the next swing, or the timing of this move changes, this indicates a variability in the dynamics of the backswing and the tension in the muscles of the right leg. This often happens when a player wants to hit a modified shot, that is an easy shot or a full shot with a particular club. A three-quarter wedge hit with a feel stroke that has no stopping point, will have greater variability, and ultimately result in greater dispersion of distances and ball locations than a more repeatable stroke that has a recognizable stopping mechanism built in.

The great ball strikers, that is, those rare players who can consistently repeat contact characteristics, resultant ball flights and shot results, are those who have either by design or chance evolved a stroke that has a secure, solid, easily reproduced stopping mechanism. A good number of these great ball strikers have fast rhythms, coupled with a lower body mechanism that prevents variability from creeping into the swing. They are the more "mechanical" players. The easy-swinging, fluid, flowing type player, whose swing is admired for appearing to be so relaxed often is plagued by great inconsistency of results, and must rely on many hours of practice, and a great short game to remain competitive. Once injured or without the motivation to practice constantly, these individuals often miss cuts, and have less than satisfying competitive results.

The Hand-Foot Concept

This approach to teaching and coaching is based on principles from a number of disciplines. In neuroanatomy, it is well known that within both the motor and sensory cortices of the brain there are large portions of gray matter assigned to the hands and feet. This permits us the opportunity to discriminate sensations to a very high degree, and to have sophisticated motor control over our hands and feet.

With this apparatus so designed for these four comparatively small parts of our bodies, it seems obvious that our teaching must focus on exactly where the hands and feet are, and what they are doing as we perform the golf swing, or any other movement for that matter. From the mechanical perspective, it is clear that we apply virtually all the forces generated by our entire body through our hands and feet. In golf, our contact for all force application is through our feet to the ground. And we transfer all our efforts to the club through our hands. Mechanically speaking, the hands and feet are the media through which we accomplish most physical activities. It makes sense then, that we focus our teaching/coaching on the hands and feet. Kinesiologically, the arrangement of our joints, myofascial tissues, and nervous system, permits us vast amounts of movement potential, with an enormous amount of dexterity, and degrees of freedom of movement in the hands and feet .This capacity brings with it both positive and negative factors. On the plus side, we can create many linkages to strike the ball with great force. With so many degrees of freedom however, there is great potential for error. In seemingly simple tasks such as putting on modern, fast greens, success depends on learning to eliminate as many degrees of freedom as possible, particularly in the hands, and to some extent, the shoulder joints. It is important then that we focus on what the hands should and should not do.

It is obvious that improving our understanding of the roles played by the hands and feet will enable us to be more effective teachers/coaches of the golf swing. Yet at the beginning of a new century, we still know almost nothing definitive about how they function, not only in the golf swing, but in most forms of physical activity. What we have to teach by are statements by great players about their *feelings* as they relate to the swing. There are no scientific studies to tell us what these players are actually doing. It has been my experience over the years that most great athletes are fully aware of what the patterns of movement required to produce an effective performance should *feel* like, but often have either wrong interpretations of their efforts, or are incapable of accurate description of what they are actually doing. If the players have simply the correct body and natural inclination for the swing and have never been forced to become fully conscious of the process, they often guess at the causes for their success. Two examples are the muscle contractions performed to initiate the backswing and the basic timing components of the swing. Even the highest-level performers have to guess which muscles actually initiate the take-away, and are unaware of the time it takes for each phase of a full golf swing. In a way it is somewhat similar to a person with *blindsight* (vision without visual consciousness) who can perform visual tasks reliably, but is totally unaware of how he is in fact able to achieve the task. The difference here of course is that the great golfer can become more aware of the performance, the person with blindsight cannot.

One reason for this, is that up to this point in time, *nobody* knows the whole story, particularly the manner in which each of the greats uses their hands and feet. Looking at V's (thumb/index finger angle), and holding the club as if you were "holding a little bird in your hands", is just a starting point. We don't know where pressure is exerted, by which fingers, or when the pressure changes occur. This information is crucial to a more complete understanding of how performers use their hands within the context of their particular swings.

Although there are excellent technologies available for determining the pressures exerted on the plantar (bottom) surfaces of the feet, only a few studies have been presented, and none that integrates this information with hand function. This topic will be discussed further in the chapter that deals with the future of golf research.

My own information regarding hands and feet is based entirely on personal experimentation and has not been subject to scientific scrutiny. In addition, I am not a professional player, so readers should judge statements in this regard with caution, and experiment with the ideas to see if the concepts work for them.

Figure 132

Tension is apparently different at each location of the body during the swing. Some muscles are fixing body parts (contracting isometrically), while others are shortening (contracting concentrically), still others may be lengthening (contracting eccentrically). In the lower right quadrant the muscles change from eccentric loading (preparatory) to concentric effort (transition and propulsion). During all of this, just what are the hands doing? And how do they affect the swing?

Earlier I wrote about the release and regripping of the club, and the variety of ways the hands can be used. Page 95 of

Cochran and Stobbs' *The Search for the Perfect Swing*, has an excellent picture and explanation of this technique. Another way to use the hands is actually not to use them. Many of the very accurate, medium distance, low ball-flight strikers basically hit the ball with little or no ulnar flexion to give the final acceleration to the clubhead. One of Nova Scotia's best players over the past 25 years has used this approach with great success. By restricting the release of the club, he always made contact with his hands 6-8 inches ahead of the ball, even with his tee shots. The loft of his driving club was more like a 2 wood to permit this position. Figure 132 shows that the hands at contact are 6-8 inches ahead of the club, and the hand speed is greater than would be expected in a typical striking pattern.

By not using the hands in the traditional manner, this golfer is able to control the clubpath much more effectively. And, provided the other contributing components have developed sufficient clubhead velocity, the golfer is able to obtain reasonable length on his drives. His usual flight path is medium to low and the face is almost always square to target long before impact. How does he accomplish this? Perhaps by maintaining constant pressure with his hands, but this of course is speculative. The notion that constant hand/finger pressure is maintained by the extremely long hitters who delay the club release is, I believe, a faulty one. The clubhead acceleration that the "late" hitters achieve cannot conceivably be attained without a vigorous set of contractions by the ulnar flexors. Evidence for this is the deceleration of the hands that occurs in front of the body prior to ball contact. If the clubhead takes the momentum, the hands have to slow down. Hand decelerations ranging from 5-8 mph are common.

The preceding material has been presented in order to demonstrate the tremendous importance of the hands and feet, and to highlight the need for more information regarding their use.

CHAPTER V

Conditioning for Golf

Over the past fifty years, there has been a steady and significant increase in the number of adults pursuing many forms of physical activity. In the early stages (1950's-1970's), a number of influential exercise scientists considered golf a poor activity choice because some of the fitness parameters such as aerobic power and strength were not adequately developed. In spite of the negativity of some of the fitness gurus, golf has gradually become one of the most popular forms of physical activity for the adult population in North America. The very reason why the experts panned this sport is one of the determinants of its amazing success. It's obvious that one doesn't need significant levels of any specific fitness parameter to play and enjoy this game. Golf is a unique experience. Weather conditions, rules, personalities, and the challenge of the game itself, set it aside from all other sports. However, the social, motivational, and emotional components of golf are not the focus of this chapter and will be left to others.

Conditioning as it relates to golf is the focus, but before a discussion of its application to this sport is ventured, basic concepts of conditioning itself would be helpful, in order to ensure that words written and words received are in sync.

I use the term 'conditioning' to refer to a program of exercises/activities performed away from the golf course. The objective is to improve, or maintain at a high level, the capacity of the body to play golf effectively without injury. By definition, these are non-specific exercises that do not involve the actual skills used in the sport. Although this form of training has been accepted and integrated into virtually all competitive sport conditioning programs, there is little evidence that much of this training actually improves performance in most sports. However, there is substantial evidence that many athletes become injured as a consequence of such training.

One major problem that occurs often is when those involved (athlete, coach, personal trainer) focus excessively on conditioning, and forget the original reason for embarking on the program. Problems emerge when objective evidence of the success of the conditioning program is expected. The athlete wants to lose body fat, increase muscle mass, lift more weight, lunge and twist with progressively heavier resistance, do more sit-ups, and chin-ups, and so on. The effort and risk-taking are simply not worth it, given the fact that there is no concrete evidence that such training actually improves sport performance. A little non-specific training *may* be helpful, but excessive training definitely is not. Athlete abuse is a problem the seriousness of which cannot be exaggerated. Those responsible for structuring conditioning programs for athletes should re-evaluate the trend that currently permeates our culture.

The philosophical bases of such a program should be:

1 To prescribe no activity that could potentially do harm to the athlete

2 To prescribe the **least** amount of any exercise that permits the athlete to perform their sport effectively, and to continually improve performance in their sport, since going for the greatest gains in the shortest amount of time often leads to injury (see graph)

3 To guide the athlete toward self-reliance, giving them an understanding of their body, technique, and training program so that they can function independently

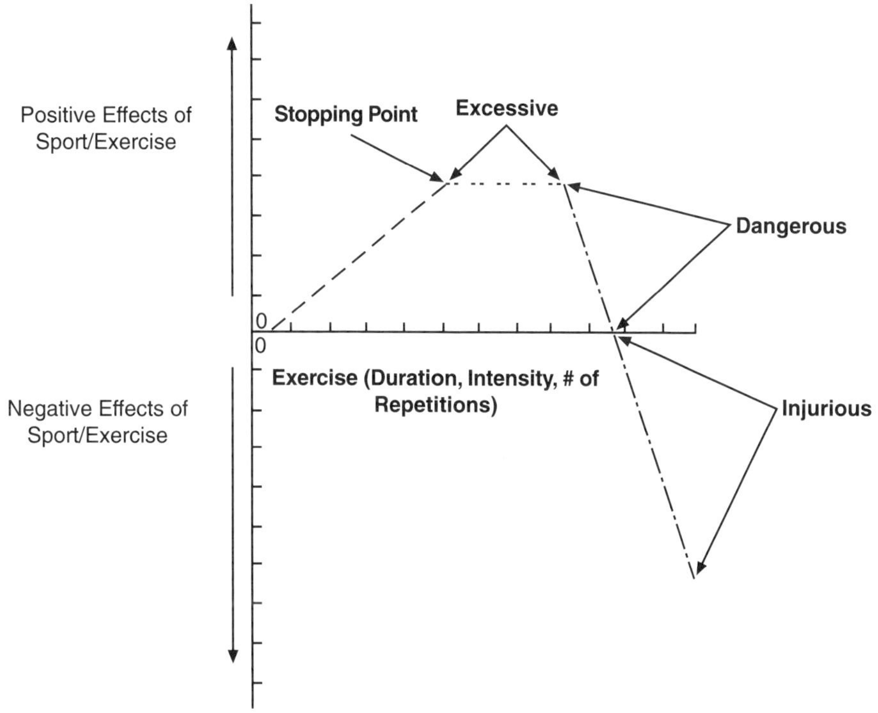

With the above principles in mind the next step is to distinguish between fitness for life (general health), physical fitness, and sport specific fitness. There is much confusion in the sporting world regarding these somewhat related, yet very different concepts. The current trend in many of the major sports is to test high-level athletes in laboratories using standard protocols (tests not specific to the sport), and making decisions regarding the training needs of the athletes based on these tests. In fact, the tests have become so important in the major professional sports that pre-season testing has become the focus of training during the off-season, and often continues during the competitive season. This, in my opinion, is one of the reasons for the vast increase in soft tissue injuries now in evidence in hockey, football, baseball, basketball, and many Olympic sports. Inappropriate cross-training, and resistance training, together with aerobic exercise that reduces tissue elasticity, have become part of virtually all conditioning programs. Interestingly, this situation has occurred in spite of evidence that this approach not only does little to improve actual sport performance, in many cases it actually detracts from it.

Because this is a strong condemnation of existing practices in sport conditioning, a few examples might prove helpful. I have personally been involved in hockey research since 1972, and have served as a consultant for a number of professional teams. I've had ample opportunity to observe the conditioning programs in this sport and experience the transition from the traditional to the modern day approach.

It is apparent to me that although the traditional conditioning approach was not ideal (the players played themselves into shape as the pre-season evolved into the regular season), they had fewer and far less severe soft tissue injuries than their modern day counterparts. In the present day, the number of game days lost to soft tissue injuries about the hip and pelvis alone is staggering. With some athletes it becomes a career-ending problem. And most of this is not only unnecessary, but is brought about by the very conditioning program designed to prevent injuries and enhance performance. The emphasis on resistance training, which produces muscle hypertrophy (increasing muscle bulk) and aerobic exercise, such as biking and jogging, often leads to both the accumulation of upper body muscle mass and the loss of tissue elasticity in the adductors, extensors and most importantly flexors of the hip joint. The added upper body mass often detracts from performance in the later stages of the second and all of the third period. It is somewhat like adding a 20-30 pound bag of sand to your chest and playing the entire game with it. The concept of course is to become bigger and stronger in order to be more effective during the "physical" parts of the game, to protect yourself from injury, and to play with more vigor throughout the game. This unfortunately does not happen. Those players whose contributions depend on quickness and endurance, and who demonstrate these qualities at their normal weight, lose these capacities when bulked-up through resistance training.

The aerobic benefit derived from exercising on a bicycle is far outweighed by the tightness that develops in the muscles that move the hip and knee joints. 45-60 minutes of stationary/moving bike training places these muscles in a shortened position and requires that they perform the repetitive movements without ever going to full extension. The injury then occurs when the athlete strides vigorously on the ice, which involves ballistically stretching the very muscles that have been shortened and tightened. This occurs in spite of the few minutes of stretching (usually static/slow stretching, which has minimal effect) intended to maintain flexibility.

A most interesting part of this unfortunate trend is that many of the hockey players who adhered scrupulously to the off-season training program and who scored highest in the general fitness testing were often the athletes most likely to injure themselves during the first few weeks of training camp. Those who played golf, swam, or enjoyed recreational activities did not score as well on the fitness tests, but often avoided the soft tissue injuries experienced by their highly motivated peers. To this day, the hockey world still has no scientific evidence that any of this non-specific training increases skating speed, shot velocity, passing/receiving skills, or any other dimension of the game. It does however, allow them to score well on the laboratory tests, and that seems these days to have become a major coaching objective.

Over the past forty years the sport of swimming has seen a similar trend. Debilitating myofascial, joint capsule, and ligamentous injuries were rare in this sport in the '50s, '60s, and early '70s, even though the mileage swum and energy expended in the pool were comparable to present-day training. The high injury rate during the latter period can be attributed to the non-specific exercise programs (dry-land training) that have become a major focus of swim coaches around the world. This in spite of the scientific evidence that has accrued over the years, that does not support this practice. For those interested in this topic I suggest visiting Coaching Science Abstracts at http://coachsci.sdsu.edu/index.htm. Dr. Brent Rushall, one of the world's pre-eminent sport scientists, has placed at this website a number of truly informative summaries of various aspects of sport science. One of the topics deals with the effect of resistance training on sport performance, and I encourage interested readers to avail themselves of this information.

If it cannot be demonstrated that intensive, non-specific training actually increases performance, one might ask why so much of it is being done. One answer may center on the need that many coaches seem to have to control more and more of the life experiences of their athletes. Another is the simple belief that if some training is good for increasing performance, then more of this "good stuff" is obviously better. In addition, exercise scientists have focused on standard laboratory tests to determine the playing fitness of athletes, and not on more specific on-site, or field tests. This, I believe, has not been helpful.

Why cover material in hockey and swimming? This is basically to show that there has been a lot of damage done to athletes by coaches and conditioning experts, and that to follow the lead of other sports may not be the best approach for golfers. Nevertheless, it appears that this trend has already taken hold in golf. I hope that those who keep records will begin an objective study on this training approach, taking into consideration that improvements in driving distance are most plausibly attributable to improved equipment, not improved conditioning.

In order to avoid semantic problems I would like to start the following section by explaining the differences between life fitness, physical fitness and sport specific fitness. This will be followed by a presentation of basic principles of exercise prescription, and finally an application of the principles to the many different groups that participate in golf.

Definitions

Life Fitness — A state of health/well-being that includes a number of physical capacities enabling an individual to participate safely and effectively in both vocational and avocational pursuits.

Physical Fitness (current model) — The physiological capacity of a variety of bodily systems to perform selected exercise protocols as measured by reliable and valid laboratory tests.

Sport Specific Fitness — The neuromuscular skills, mental aptitude, and physiological capacity to perform in a sport. The latter is more related to, and dependent on life fitness than it is physical fitness.

Physiological Components of Fitness (General)

Aerobic Endurance — The capacity to sustain whole-body activity through the transport and utilization of oxygen.

Anaerobic Energy — The capacity for muscular work at intensities above that which can be supplied by aerobic metabolism.

Muscular Endurance — The capacity to sustain large work output in localized muscle groups.

Muscular Strength — The capacity to exert force in a single continuous contraction (activation).

Muscular Power — The capacity to exert force in a given amount of time. This can be further divided into a number of categories, such as instantaneous power against high resistance (vertical jump), or instantaneous power against light resistance (golf drive). Although there are several other examples of muscular power, they will not be discussed here.

Flexibility — The capacity of body tissues to allow, without injury, excursions at a joint or group of joints.

Each sport, or activity type within a sport, has its own set of physiological demands. Marathon running demands high levels of aerobic endurance, pain tolerance, running skill, and an ectomorphic body type. It is quite obvious that most of the world's best performers in this event would not score well on many of the standard tests of physical fitness. Upper body strength, power, and general flexibility, are some of the tests that would render their overall fitness scores to be average or below. On the other hand, specialists in sprinting, high jump, or the hammer throw, have quite different demands on their bodies and therefore should prepare specifically for their chosen events. The body types, neuromuscular arrangements, mental preparation, and so on, are different for each sport, and the training should reflect those differences. Athletes from each of these sub-disciplines within track and field would tend to score quite differently on tests of physical fitness.

Application to Golf

How does this apply to golf? How well does one have to score on the standard, general fitness tests to be able to play and enjoy this game? Without venturing into a sophisticated discussion, let's simply examine how the game is played in order to establish some of the parameters, then look at some of the world's best players to see how our cursory analysis holds up.

The greatest percentage of active time on the golf course is spent walking and standing. For a typical foursome to complete a four-hour round, the speed is moderate and at times slow, with numerous stoppages for shot making. This means that although the aerobic energy demands are quite mild, each player must have the capacity to handle them without undue strain. One should not be panting over the ball while making a stroke. Interspersed with the walking are the strokes taken to move the ball toward each green. They involve the participation of a large number of muscles (as previously discussed) contracting strongly under conditions of rapid stretch. This aspect of the game is more likely to produce injuries than all other parts combined, and perhaps should be the focus of an intelligent conditioning program. Of considerable importance is that the player must be able to cope with the environmental demands while walking and striking the ball. Taken together with whatever mind/body stress is imposed from within during the game, a round of golf can be a tiring, even demanding experience.

One needs to have at least a moderate level of walking aerobic endurance, a capacity to endure the elements, and the tissue elasticity and resiliency to take many aggressive swings at the ball. What other components are needed? Great muscular strength, high anaerobic power, or large capacity for local muscular endurance? Not really. One doesn't even need an increased capacity for flexibility to play the game. However, as we'll soon discuss, this is the key ingredient to improving your physiological capacity to strike the ball effectively. Without it however, one can still participate in and enjoy the game.

Although the previous discussion is but a cursory look at the fitness parameters required for golf, let's apply what has been discussed to the top players in the world today. What stands out initially is the vast array of body types (somatotypes) that are seen on the three main professional tours in North America. This is one factor that sets golf apart from most other sports. How can the ectomorphic, the rotund, and the well-muscled all play professional golf? It is because they all have the skills necessary, at least the minimum amount of aerobic endurance, weather tolerance capacity, and the emotional intelligence needed to play the game effectively under pressure. It would also be helpful if the player were in reasonably good general health at the time of competition. However, many great rounds of golf have been played by individuals with significant illnesses.

Without actual test data to rely on, I will venture the opinion that laboratory fitness levels on the tours vary considerably and that this factor is not significantly correlated to earnings or wins. In spite of this, I sense that there is movement toward the new physical fitness approach being applied to professional golfers. It is my opinion that this trend will lead to the same types of problems experienced in the other professional sports, should the "gurus" place great emphasis on strength training, bicycle riding, and other inappropriate cross-training activities.

Since golf is enjoyed by millions of people of all ages, from all walks of life, and in varying degrees of health, a discussion of conditioning for this sport will best be approached segmentally, that is, by groupings.

Youngsters-This is by far the easiest group to discuss insofar as exercise prescription for golf is concerned. For the vast majority of pre-adolescent children the very opportunity to have access to a golf facility, to receive basic instruction, and be permitted to practice and play, is enough activity related to golf. This, together with their physical education program at school, and regular participation in vigorous play, should be sufficient to keep them healthy and prepared to play golf. However, current trends indicate a significant increase in the number of obese children in North America, and this has vast implications for school administrators, physical education and recreation specialists, and coaches of all sports, including golf. This does not mean that an overweight child has little chance to excel at this game, because a quick look at the tours will show that many of the world's best golfers are considerably above their ideal weight.

Teenagers-These individuals are all going through significant anatomical, hormonal, and social changes. Although this phase of life presents many challenges, one attribute that most teenagers have, particularly when motivated, is energy. Another is tissue resiliency, that is, they can perform a vast array of activities and experience less soreness and lasting pain than adults can. If afforded the opportunity to practice and play golf, most can stay at it for long periods of time, shaping their skills, and developing the physical attributes necessary to play well. Teenagers, as well as youngsters, do not need non-specific training programs (such as aerobics, strength training, etc.). In fact, this is one period when too much concentration on strength training can have a negative effect. This will soon be discussed more fully.

Adult Women–This segment of the golfing world has grown rapidly over the past decade and merits significant attention. The emergence of the LPGA, WNBA, and other high profile sports, together with enlightened legislation, has led to an explosion of female participation in sport, and from most perspectives this has been an excellent advance. However, as women's sport becomes more and more competitive, it seems that there is much borrowing from male training practices, and evidence is accumulating that injury rates among competitive female athletes in a number of sports is increasing at an alarming rate. It is my hope that this trend will be reversed through an intelligent application of knowledge regarding the differences between the sexes, particularly the myofascial and ligamentous tolerances that predispose women to tissue failure when training becomes excessive and the loads result in injury. One example is the inordinate number of ACL (anterior cruciate ligament) surgeries that have been performed over the past decade as a result of injuries sustained in basketball, volleyball, soccer, and other sports. Excessive use of plyometrics, heavy resistance training involving full squats, stationary cycling for long periods of time, inappropriate cross-training, together with exceptionally long and arduous practices are some of the likely reasons for this alarming increase in sport injuries among women.

How then do we approach conditioning for women interested in playing golf? First and foremost, it is important to maintain an excellent state of general health. It is a fact that we generally do things better and appreciate them more if we are in a good state of health. Sufficient sleep, nutritious food, and reasonable control over life's stresses and strains, are the most critical factors, and are excellent topics for future discussion. However, I will assume that these factors are in place and concentrate on those physical components that relate specifically to golf.

Aerobics

Referring back to the previous discussion, it is clear that walking should be emphasized all year round. If the footing is safe, a mixture of hills and uneven terrain, which best resembles a typical golf course, would be ideal. In the off-season (if you have one), an hour per day, covering three to four miles would be sufficient. This approach could be maintained throughout the playing season if you regularly ride in a motorized cart on the links. Should you live where climatic conditions often preclude walking outside, then a treadmill would suffice. The use of steppers and climbers as an adjunct to walking should not be overdone. Many individuals develop lumbo-sacral, sacro-iliac and other problems if they spend too much time on these devices, particularly women over forty. Excessive walking on the treadmill when it is set at a severe grade may also lead to injury for many. Moderation in both distance covered and intensity level, plus proper hydration are key to a positive aerobic workout for golfers. If climatic conditions and personal preference indicate cross-country skiing, or snow-shoeing, these are excellent winter options that will enhance the golfer's aerobic system and contribute to upper body strength and muscular endurance. The judicious use of a cross-country simulator can also yield similar benefits, should opportunity or weather conditions preclude outdoor participation. I would caution golfers to avoid the use of a stationary bike as the preferred aerobic training device. Although it will improve circulo-respiratory efficiency, it has another effect that is undesirable, the shortening and tightening of many important muscle groups, such as the hamstrings and hip flexors. This, together with the constant and undesirable pressure from the seat, and the fact that the aerobic benefits can be gained from other less harmful activities, is the reason why I do not recommend biking as either cross-training for any sport, or for general aerobic conditioning.

Disabled and injured golfers who must use a cart to play each round of golf should consider doing their cardiovascular training in water. Aquatic aerobics, swimming laps, and deep water walking or running (page 90), are all excellent exercise options.

Strength

This factor is often singled out as the most deficient physical component of aspiring female golfers. Some experts identify the hands specifically, others the upper body, still others point to a general overall weakness. Yet, one never sees data to support these contentions. What is clear however, is that many outstanding female golfers appear not to possess high levels of strength, yet can hit the ball a long way. It will continue to be confusing until someone actually measures the relevant strength components and determines the level of association between this factor and the creation of clubhead velocity. How much hand or upper body strength is needed to contribute significantly to the acceleration of the clubhead? It is my contention that research will demonstrate a low to moderate correlation between these two factors.

The previous statements are not intended to stop women from doing resistance exercises. If it is deemed appropriate for an individual to include resistance work in their daily program, the only recommendation I have is to avoid the tendency to focus on low repetition/high resistance workouts. This, to be sure, will lead to faster strength gains, but will also predispose the participant to injury. There have been, and will continue to be, significant numbers of athletes injured during heavy resistance training. Many repetitions (twenty to thirty), performed to full range, with light to moderate resistance, done at slow speeds constitutes the safest, and surest approach. Typical workout programs for the major muscle groups of the body can be found at any fitness club, gymnasium, or other location where people are active. However there are many popular exercises prescribed by trainers that can cause or predispose the golfer to injury. Appendix A contains a number of contraindicated exercises together with safer options for some of the targeted muscle groups.

Flexibility

As with other physical characteristics, each individual has a personal capacity for creating range of motion at or about a joint or series of joints. Although many women may have sufficient flexibility for creating the necessary movements required to accelerate the clubhead to the desired velocities, many do not know how to employ these movement excursions. A frequently used swing pattern for women begins with a faulty preparatory phase (Figures 133 and 134). The club is lifted by means of shoulder joint and shoulder girdle movements to the completion of the backswing. There is little or no thoracic rotation, or subsequent pelvic rotation.

Without stretching the large muscles of the back and pelvis, there can be no expectation of high clubhead velocity during the propulsive phase. The above movement pattern indicates

Figure 133

Figure 134

a lack of conscious proprioception (muscle and joint awareness) and conscious motor control, not necessarily a lack of flexibility in the thorax and pelvis.

Many women have not experienced the movement patterns necessary for the full golf swing. The learning of these motions is often hindered when the very beginning of instruction involves striking the golf ball, rather than developing proper motion sequences, and subsequently applying the learned patterns to striking the ball. What generally happens is that the learner is told to keep the head still, and focus on the ball throughout the swing. This objective is best accomplished by the pattern of movement just discussed. The head remains still, but the resulting swing is ineffective.

I believe that the reason for this common movement pattern is that women generally are more receptive students than men. They usually begin lessons at an earlier stage, listen carefully to instructions, and try in good faith to follow them. Unfortunately, this often leads to restricted patterns, particularly in a unique sport such as golf, where there is often little or no transfer of motor skills from their previous sport experiences.

As is often the case in sport, learning the correct movements is usually hindered by holding all instruction in the actual sport setting or by asking beginners to learn as they play. This often severely restricts the learning process for most people, and only the few truly gifted and adventurous youngsters continue to improve their skills and progressively add to their repertoire. By having the beginner, particularly the adult, observe the outcome (where the ball goes), rather than focus on the movement patterns that will eventually lead to successful ball striking, teachers inadvertently shape the swing in a way not intended. However, this is not the topic at hand, and I will leave teaching methodologies for another time and place.

As previously discussed, trunk and shoulder flexibility (thoracic rotation, shoulder girdle and joint mobility) are important contributors to the creation of maximum velocity in the full golf swing. If an individual has such flexibility, then shaping the lessons to integrate these capabilities into the swing is the objective. If more flexibility is necessary, then I recommend the following exercises.

The protocol for developing flexibility presented here is based on the physiological principle called "reversal of antagonists", a very specific procedure, which is part of a larger exercise program referred to as Proprioceptive Neuromuscular Facilitation (PNF). In my book *Scientific Stretching for Sport-3S*, (1973), a simple planar (two-dimensional) method for applying the reversal of antagonists technique was explained, and illustrations were presented to show the reader how to use this method of stretching tissue*. Since our first study in 1969 and continuing up to the present day, our research and studies from other labs, have consistently shown this approach to be three times as effective as either slow or fast/ballistic stretching, and the results last longer. In fact, it is more effective than alternative PNF stretching methods as well. Full reversal of antagonists following the procedure presented below is the best method for increasing tissue elasticity, and as a result improving flexibility.

* A new text, *Flexibility: A Comprehensive Guide,* will be published soon.

Before describing the exercises, it is important for the reader to understand that limits to range of motion can be caused by a number of body tissues. Some examples are the bone to bone contact as seen in elbow extension, soft tissue contact as seen in elbow flexion, tightness of ligaments as seen in knee extension, and myofascial tightness (muscle and its connective tissue) as seen in hip flexion with an extended knee. Most people are of the belief that it is muscle tissue itself that is responsible for restricting range of motion. However, when soft tissue is the restricting agent, it is usually the fascia, or the connective tissue that envelops the muscle tissue that is the cause (epimysium, perimysium, and endomysium). This is an important distinction, because a number of flexibility exercises including slow or static stretching (held for five to twenty seconds), the most popular of all methods, does little to effect change in this connective tissue, and as a result, yields very small gains in range. The limited gains are often lost during many forms of exercise and/or inactivity. This information is based on over 30 years of research into flexibility carried out in the Sport Science Lab at Dalhousie University, and can be found in the articles listed in my CV (curriculum vitae).

The most effective way to elicit a release and stretch of the fascia and its enveloped muscle is to perform a series of maneuvers that involve contracting both the muscle group to be stretched and its antagonists (opposites). Figure 135 shows the starting position for a 3S exercise to stretch the left triceps (long head), left posterior deltoid, left teres major, left latissimus dorsi, left rhomboids and left middle trapezius.

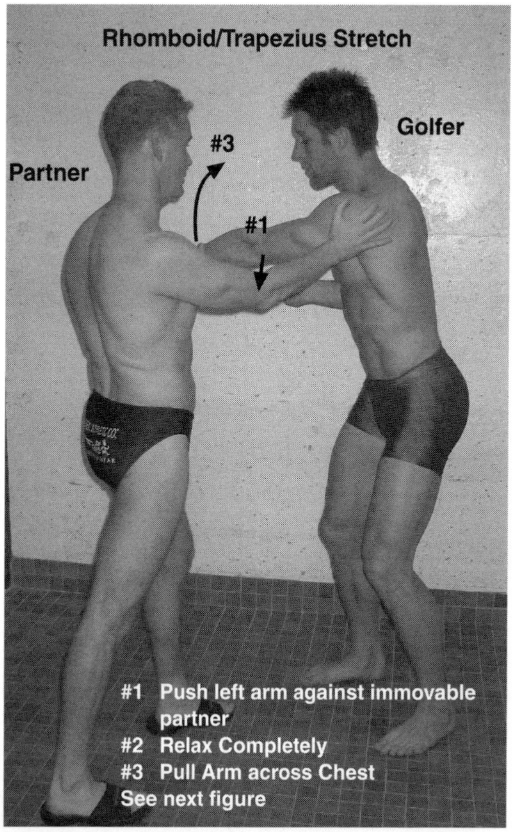

Figure 135

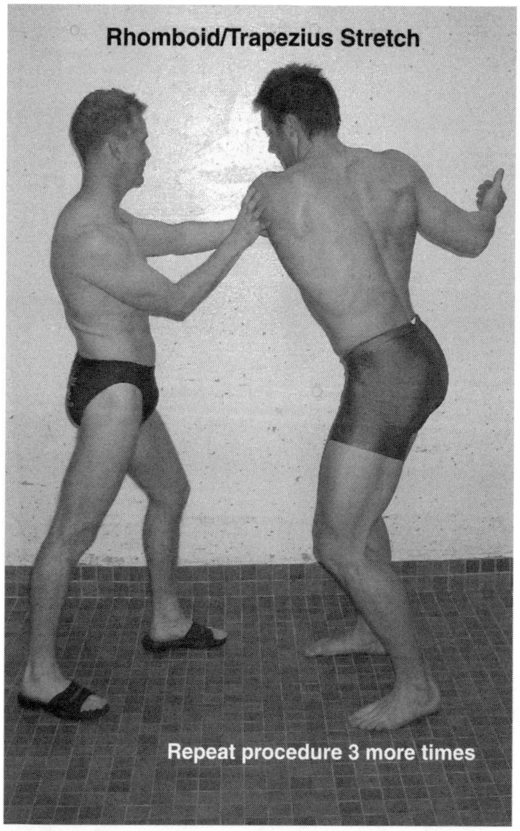

Figure 136

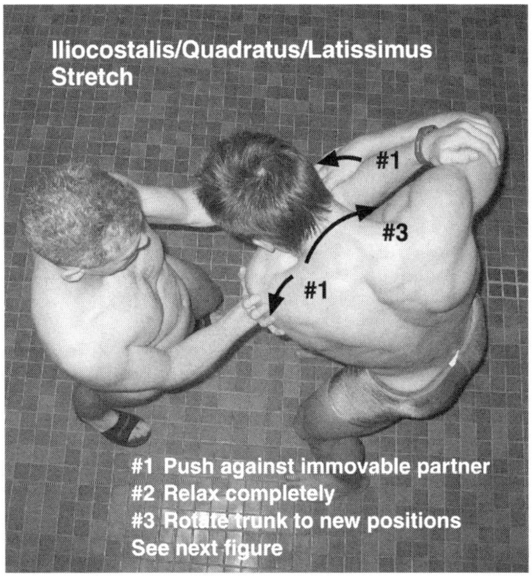

Figure 137

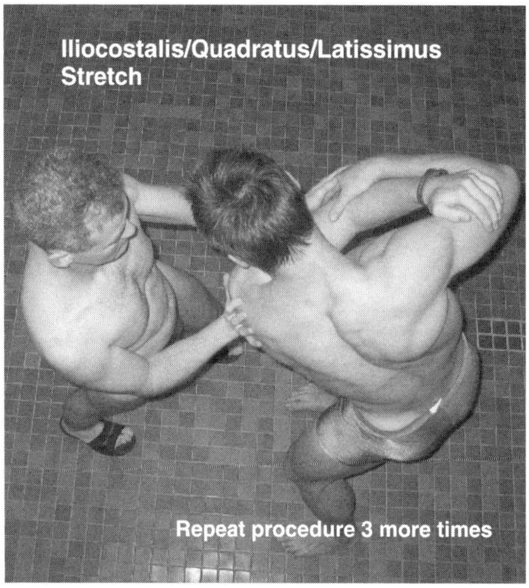

Figure 138

Once in a lengthened position, rather than holding for a period of time, the golfer actively attempts to pull the arm downward thereby contracting these muscles against the immovable force of the partner, producing an isometric contraction (activation). A gradual build-up of effort is begun and once a strong but not excessive (50%) activation is reached it is held for six seconds, (four second increase, six second hold).

This is followed by a complete relaxation of these muscles, and an activation of the antagonists, the left (pectoralis major, anterior deltoid). With less resistance from the agonist, the golfer can pull the limb to a further range of motion with the left arm antagonists, and can get assistance with a light lifting effort from the partner, as seen in Figure 136 (five seconds in all, relax for two seconds, reposition for three). Four repetitions of this sequence will take one minute.

Figure 137 shows the starting position for a 3S exercise to stretch the left quadratus lumborum, ilio-costalis lumborum, lower longissimus, and latissimus dorsi muscles. This specifically targets the muscles and their fascia that might contribute to restricting the separation of upper (thorax/chest) and lower (pelvis and legs) body previously described. Once the golfer has assumed the starting position, which is basically the stance for hitting a full drive coupled with rotation of the upper body to the point where pelvic rotation starts, the partner then assumes the position depicted and prevents the arms and upper body of the golfer from moving back to the start position while the golfer performs the exercise sequence. This is similar to the first exercise in that it begins with a contraction that would, if not resisted, rotate the golfer back to the start or neutral position. Resistance by the partner prevents any movement from taking place. The golfer gradually increases the activation until a mild (25% effort) is achieved (four second build-up). This effort is held for a further six seconds, and is followed by a full relaxation of these muscles, and contraction of the antagonists to pull the upper trunk to a more rotated position (Figure 138). This can be aided by light pressure

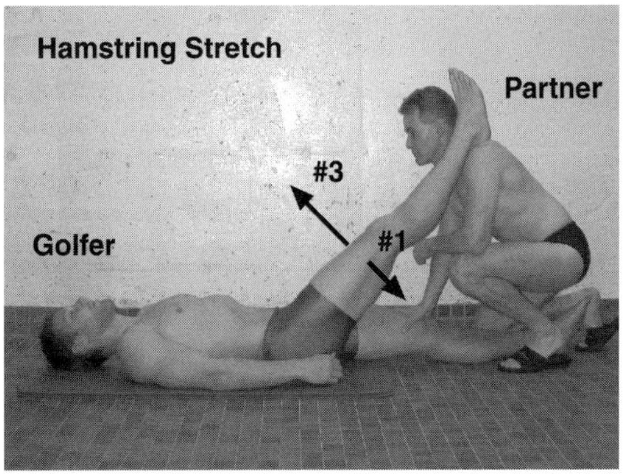

Figure 139 **#1 Push down against immovable partner (isometric contraction)**
#2 Relax completely
#3 Pull leg up to new position (flex hip)
See next figure

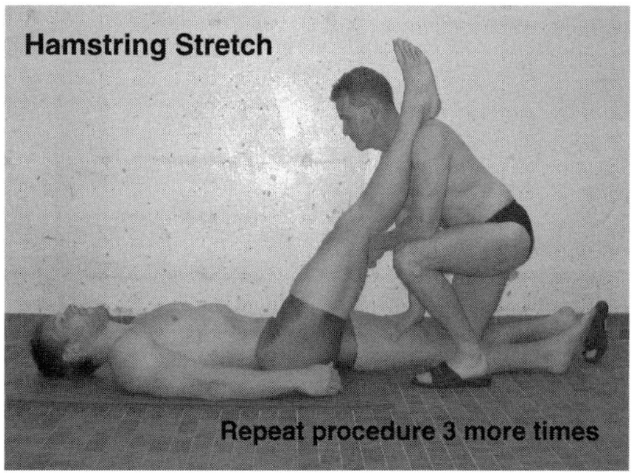

Figure 140

from the partner. This is then performed another three times. The total time for these two stretches (arm and back) is two minutes.

For those who have tight hamstrings with its accompanying problems, Figures 139 and 140 show a 3S exercise for stretching this very important muscle group. Once the golfer has been positioned with one leg lifted (hip flexion) with the knee straight, the partner assumes the kneeling position indicated in order to resist the contractions of the golfer who is going to try to pull the leg down to the ground by contracting the stretched hamstrings. The partner resists while the golfer gradually builds a strong but not excessive (50%) contraction taking four seconds, then holds the desired level for an additional six, relaxes the hamstrings completely, then contracts the hip flexors concentrically to pull the leg to a more stretched position. This can be done by the golfer completely, or aided by very light pressure from the partner. Once again the procedure is repeated another three times for best results.

Maximum contractions are not necessary to elicit excellent improvements in elasticity of these tissues. For younger golfers and those with no history of back problems, a gradual increase in the force of the isometric contractions will enhance the effect. However, I do not recommend strong contractions (over 50%) for the back exercise, or excessive contractions (over 80%) for any other area of the body.

Positive results will be seen and felt from the first set of exercises. It must be remembered that these effects, like all physiological parameters, will last only for so long, and then must be re-applied. Serious golfers will get benefits that will be more lasting and effective if they perform these three stretches each day prior to play or practice, and if possible, afterward.

Stretching exercises for most of the lower body musculature can be done alone, with a partner, or on a mechanized device of my design that is shown in Figures 141-144.

As an alternative to 3S stretching, I recommend that golfers consider yoga. It is the best form of slow stretching, and if done properly, very safe. Three or four poses would cover the hamstrings, trunk rotators, and shoulder musculature previously discussed.

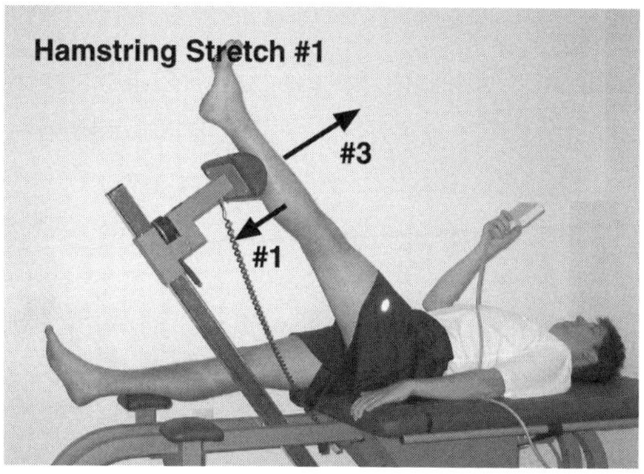

Figure 141 #1 Push against immovable pad
#2 Relax completely
#3 Pull leg up to new position
See next figure

Figure 142 Repeat procedure 3 more times

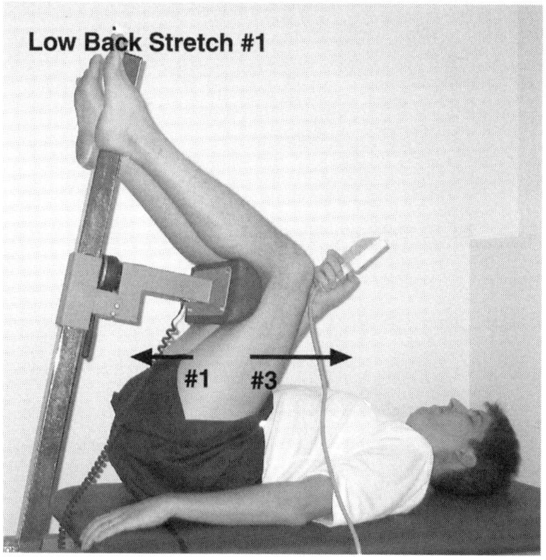

Figure 143 #1 Push gently against immovable pad
#2 Relax completely
#3 Pull legs closer to chest
See next figure

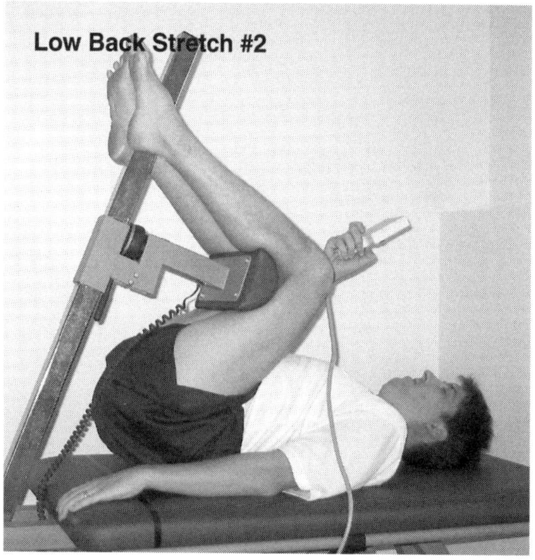

Figure 144 Repeat procedure 3 more times

Adult men - This group has always made up the largest segment of the golfing community. The level of general health and specific fitness for this sport was essential in the era prior to the motorized cart, for all participants had to walk the course, as well as perform the strokes. Although many of the early golfers had the advantage of a caddy, a significant number, particularly the younger men, carried their clubs. The loss of caddies is, in my view, lamentable. It seemed to be a good thing for all concerned. It allowed the youngsters the opportunity to earn money, provide a service, and learn about the game, rules, and social graces. It provided the players with the opportunity to play the game unhindered, to walk the course easily, enjoy the social interaction with playing partners, and to pick up information from those caddies with experience. Although it is looked upon by some as a means to enhance the exercise experienced while playing a round of golf, I think that many, particularly those over forty, should think twice before deciding to carry their own clubs.

Having gone through this phase, I noticed in my mid-forties that the strain from continually lifting and lowering the clubs started to affect both my fatigue level, and ultimately the quality of my strokes. Soreness following play was increased as well as residual discomfort the following morning. It is not by chance that serious amateur and virtually all professional players have caddies. A battery operated club caddy is an excellent alternative, which permits the player the opportunity to walk the course, yet not experience the strain of carrying, and it's something that I've found truly enhances the golfing experience. The fact that active youngsters can not only carry their clubs, but do so while playing continuously for more than one round of golf exemplifies the point regarding both the energy and the tissue resiliency of most youth. However, those who decide to carry their clubs, whether young or old, would be wise to use an ultralight bag, carry fewer clubs, little extra equipment, and use a harness that distributes the weight evenly across the low back. For men, as for women, maintaining a high level of general health is the most important ingredient if one is to participate and enjoy this game. Attention to the quality of food, sleep, and the environment are essential. However, we shall now return to the physiological factors specifically related to playing the game.

Aerobics

Although, as previously mentioned, there appear to be differences between men and women in response to extremes in training, I do not believe that this applies to foundational aerobic exercise. Therefore, my recommendation is that the men follow the same type of program for aerobic training that was mentioned earlier for women. Readily available opportunities to walk, the specificity of the exercise to golf, and the positive contribution it makes to one's general health, are all excellent reasons to continue a year-round walking program. Other forms of aerobic exercise can be beneficial as well. I particularly recommend walking and running in deep water when either injury or environmental conditions don't permit outdoor exercise. Figures 145-147 illustrate the position and movement patterns of this activity.

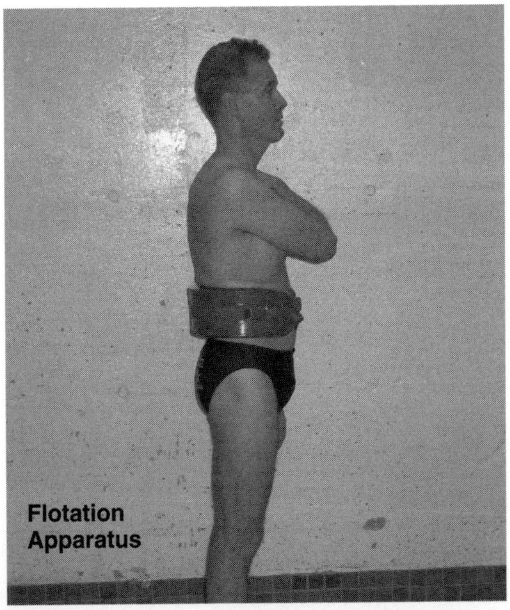

Figure 145

Figure 146

Full range of motion for the joints of the lower limb, some upper body participation in the overall movement pattern, capacity to elevate aerobic intensity, and the soothing nature of the water, are all benefits of this activity. The only possible contraindications for this exercise would be a sensitivity to the chemicals in the pool, or a water phobia.

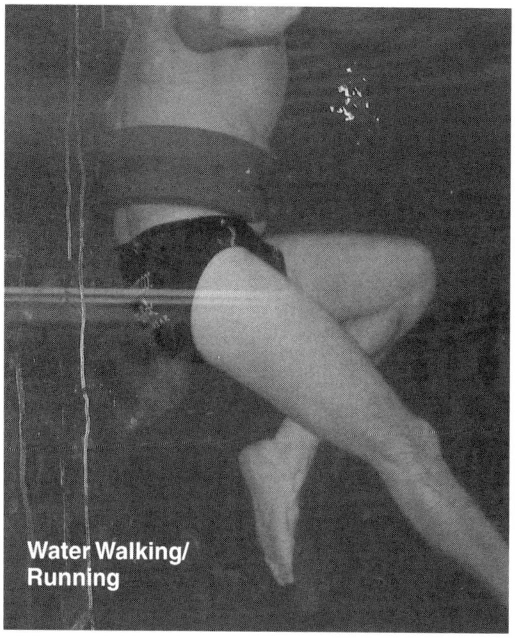

Figure 147

Strength

This is a topic of great interest to many. Fitness experts are pushing strength training for everyone, and they have some reasons and scientific support for such a position. However, with many aspects of our lives, some participation and level of intensity in an activity may be a good thing, but excess often isn't. Training done slowly, with full range of motion, using low to moderate resistance over many repetitions (20-30), will lead to moderate strength gains and increases in local muscular endurance. This can be accomplished with little risk of injury, and allow for an enjoyable workout. High resistance, low repetition training will lead to greater strength gains, and add more muscle mass. However, the potential for incurring an injury is far greater with this approach. This statement is not without foundation, as many elite athletes have suffered serious insults to their soft tissues while training in the gym. In addition, exercises such as full squats, leg presses, dead lifts, and so on, performed at high resistances, often predispose the athlete to injury later when they are training in their sport. Repeatedly exposing tendons, ligaments, vertebral discs and menisci to compressive and shear forces may cause sufficient microtearing to encourage a full-blown injury to the tissue when going through a normal training workout.

The average golfer should understand all the issues before embarking on an intensive strength-training program. What is the risk/benefit ratio of the training program? How much time, effort and money will go into such a program, and what possible benefits and other effects can be expected? Will I be able to hit the ball farther? How will I be able to apply this newly developed strength? How much training will I have to do to maintain this level of strength throughout the golfing season?

Another complication is that of added bulk, even if it is in the form of muscle. Small amounts of hypertrophy together with some fat loss, developed over a reasonable time period, can be a positive thing. Large amounts of muscle tissue in strategic locations can hinder the movement patterns, alter the momentum transfers, and change the rhythm of the golfer's swing. Added strength is far outweighed by the negative effects of excessive muscularity. A quick glance at the longer hitters on any of the tours does not reveal heavily muscled individuals, as has already been discussed. Pound for pound, the longest hitters on the PGA tour are Hank Kuehne, Charles Howell and Jeff Sluman, and a number of others who at very light body weight can equal or surpass many of their heavier, stronger colleagues.

Consider that all the players on the LPGA tour can outdrive the vast majority of male golfers. Strength testing would likely reveal that most men hold a distinct advantage over these pros, whether measuring leg strength or, more significantly, upper body strength. Surely it is clear that superior strength per se is not an important criterion when evaluating the capacity to accelerate a light object such as a golf club. Those in other sports who have gone this route have not found the transfer to be what they expected, and many have been injured in their attempts. Over the past few years a number of touring pros have started serious conditioning programs. I would venture that most who've gone to excess and altered their basic body characteristics, really stressing the strength component, do not hit the ball any farther than they did prior to the non-specific training. Some may have actually lost distance. Remember that one must take into account the effects of the new golf equipment. In order to truly test the effect of any conditioning program, one must compare an individual's performance using the same equipment before and after training. Another way to evaluate this effect is to compare performance outcomes before and after the conditioning programs. Wins, world rankings, scoring average, driving distance and accuracy, greens in regulations etc. would reveal something about the possible total effects of these programs. Such an investigation, I believe, would show that the effects for most are negligible. Some will have improved, but more than likely, many will have performed at a lower level.

A brief word on one of the trends now practiced by a number of elite sport athletes: ballistic resistance training. This involves rapid contractions of the large muscles of the body against significant resistance. Plyometric jump training for volleyball and basketball is an example of this approach. Throwing medicine balls while vigorously turning or flexing the torso would be another example, applied to the trunk musculature. Swinging a very heavy golf club at high speed would be another. My view is that these exercises should be approached with caution by elite golfers, and extreme caution by the average person. The possibility of serious injury is ever present. There is a point when performing ballistic sport movements, at which any added resistace encountered, particularly at the transition phases of the skills, could tear soft tissue. Young, physically gifted, superior athletes are sometimes injured by these types of training. What does that mean for the rest of the population? Considering that it may not improve your swing at all, does it seem the prudent thing to do? I think not, and recommend caution if you decide this approach is for you.

For the vast majority of golfers a mild to moderate resistance program as outlined will serve best, prevent severe injuries from occurring during training, and help prevent them while golfing. This program can be completed at home using light weights, or at any fitness facility, gymnasium, or other activity center. For contraindicated exercises, see Appendix A.

Flexibility

This is a most important factor for men to consider adding to their exercise program. Often they need this training more than women, who tend to be more flexible. Tightness in hamstrings, low back, chest and shoulder girdle, are among the problems to be focused on. The exercises already explained and illustrated above would be the essential three.

It should be kept in mind that this stretching protocol is not only more effective than traditional slow stretching, it can be applied specifically to those areas most involved with the golf swing. It is also safe if the person follows the exercise prescription exactly. The slow build-up of the isometric contraction that is part of all 3S exercises, allows the golfer time to stop the contraction should they feel any discomfort. 3S exercises are never to be done rapidly, or in a forced manner, and the partner is never to exert more than the lightest of pressures during the elongation phase (further stretching). This way they are always performed in a safe manner, with all the benefits, and little risk. As previously mentioned (page 88) Yoga is an excellent alternative to 3S stretching.

It is my view that the simple exercise program presented here will accomplish all the important conditioning objectives for the average golfer. This, together with practicing health generating behaviors that are part of one's lifestyle, will enable the golfer to more fully enjoy the game, and perhaps even to improve their playing ability.

Pre-Game Warm-up

The following routine is designed to prepare the player gently and safely for a round of golf. Adhering to the above principles, these exercises will prepare the soft tissues for golf-specific activity, without putting excessive demands on the body.

Walk- Begin with a short 5 minute walk about the facility, ending with one minute of walking up and down a set of stairs.

Chipping and Putting- As much pre-game practice time as you deem necessary.

Prior to Tee-Off

Exercise #1- Stretching the lower body. Standing erect with a club across the low back area (Figures 148 -149), gently rotate the entire body to the right and left to end range. Ten cycles of this exercise (30-40 seconds) will stretch the soft tissues and joint capsules about the hips, knees and ankles.

Exercise #2- Stretching the trunk. After assuming the lower body/trunk set-up position used for ball-striking, place a club across the upper back, under the armpits, and secured at the elbows (Figures 150-151). Gently rotate the thorax and pelvis to the right and left to end range. Ten cycles of this exercise (30-40 seconds) will stretch the soft tissues responsible for trunk rotation, and the facet joints of the thoracic vertebrae.

Figure 148

Figure 149

Figure 150

Figure 151

Figure 152

Figure 153

Exercise #3- Stretching the Shoulder Girdle and Trunk. Assume the same lower body/ trunk position as in exercise #2, with a club across the top of the shoulder blades (Figures 152-153). Gently rotate the upper trunk and pelvis to the right and left to end range while applying light pressure with the hands to help pull the shoulder girdle into stretch at the end of each range. Ten cycles of this exercise (30-40 seconds) will prepare the shoulder girdle musculature for ball striking.

Figure 154

Exercise #4- Stretching the Shoulder Joint. Standing erect with a club in one hand, simply rotate the arm slowly in a full circular motion at the shoulder (Figure 154). Five forward and five backward motions for each shoulder would be sufficient.

Exercise #5- Stretching the forearms and wrists- Standing erect with a club held in a normal grip, alternately perform radial flexion and ulnar flexion (Figure 155-156). Five repetitions would be sufficient. This should be followed by five repetitions of pronation/supination performed while the wrists are radially flexed, (Figure 157-158)

Exercise #6- A series of full practice swings would serve as the final preparation for the drive from the first tee. They should be progressive, building up gradually to full swing intensity.

The above exercises should take very little time, and yet should adequately prepare the player for a full round of golf. These exercises may also be used within the conditioning program.

Figure 155

Figure 156

Figure 157

Figure 158

CHAPTER VI

Improving Our Understanding of Golf

It is doubtful that a significant improvement in the playing ability of most golfers will take place through either an evolutionary process or through current approaches to golf instruction. One reason for this is that practicing the game itself, with immediate attention to score, rather than to the movements that created the score, usually leads to a restriction of patterns rather than an exploration of the wide variety of possible ways to deal with the situations that occur during the game. This phenomenon can also be seen in sports like hockey and baseball, where most children now experience these activities almost exclusively in regimented and formalized settings. Two-hour improvisations of one on one shinny, or five-player rotational stickball, scrub, or any other variation of baseball/softball are hardly ever seen, yet were the norm just one generation ago.

In years past children developed many of their sport skills through seemingly endless hours of play, that included making up their own modifications of various sports so that they could enjoy the activity alone, one on one, or in small groups. This exploration through creative play, together with later formalized instruction on the entire set of skills of the game, without subjecting the children to game pressures is perhaps the best approach. It is not, however, the way things are typically done in North America. It might be an explanation for why so many Europeans are now being drafted for play in the NHL, and why so many Caribbean ballplayers make up such a large portion of the Majors.

Another possible reason for the skill level not advancing, is that in spite of the volumes that have been written, the plethora of videos and CD's, the instruction available on the Golf Channel and elsewhere on TV, and some biomechanics research devoted to golf, we still don't know very much about it. The external movements of the great players have been analyzed so often that the devotees really believe they know what is taking place as the swing is performed. However, when delving deeper, it is clear that little is known about how the movements are actually brought about, that is, the internal mechanisms and their effect on behavior. For example, we know nothing about grip pressure. We are told what the players *think* the grip pressure is when they swing, but we know that this ballistic movement occurs in such a way as to make this type of feedback difficult to interpret. Some great golfers actually believe that they don't bring about a contraction of the ulnar flexors when the club is accelerated, that gravity and centrifugal force cause this effect. What if they are wrong, and many golfers who are trying to perform the swing with no effort from their forearms, are actually hindering their performance? Does grip pressure remain constant throughout the swing, does one hand squeeze harder than the other for one type of backswing, and the reverse for a second type of backswing? No one knows the answers, because we have not done the research to find out.

As crucial as the hands are to almost everything we do in life, and particularly in a sport such as golf, it is amazing to think that we know virtually nothing about these anatomical wonders. What about the feet, then, those parts that truly separate humanity from the rest of the animal kingdom (no other animals, primates included, have such structures)? We know a bit more about them because of the equipment that has been developed to measure pressure and forces created at the foot-ground interface. Shoe manufacturers have an obvious interest and a number of companies have developed excellent devices for measuring these forces. A few golfers have been analyzed, and this has been helpful, but we still don't know how this information applies to different types of swings, whether or not there is some force curve that applies across the board to all swings, or how the foot information relates to the hands, or to the body musculature as it is selectively firing to perform the swing pattern.

This is another area where little is known. A few studies scattered in some journals have looked at the electromyography (electrical activity of muscle) of a few golfers during the full golf swing. Some focus on injury analysis, others on rehabilitation, few actually deal with how the full swing is performed, and why an individual is successful with the muscle patterns they have selected. They do not tell us what muscles initiate what particular type of backswing, when and how forcefully they contract in order to get the club into position for the transition and downswing. And of course, there is also little or no useful information on the latter two phases of the swing. Obviously, when a great player performs very rapid preparation, transition, and propulsive phases the muscle contractions will have to be quite different from those of the slow, languid swing pattern. But how they differ, and how to use such information to teach beginning golfers have yet to be determined.

In my view, these gaps in knowledge, and the negative effects they have on teaching, can be filled by establishing kinesiology laboratories that focus exclusively on golf-related research. Present emphasis on purely biomechanical parameters should be blended with information about the musculature of the body, with particular attention to the forces generated by the hands and feet. Large numbers of both male and female golfers, ranging in ability and age, should be studied, the data then statistically analyzed in order to account for variances in performance. This information should then be used to develop teaching strategies that would emphasize individual needs and tendencies. The teaching would, in essence, be based on the learner's profile, specifically their movement patterns and innate neuromuscular capacities.

How would such a laboratory be set up? What equipment would be needed? The following list would enable a research team to accomplish the objectives stated above.

1 — 15-20 channel EMG telemetry system. This would allow simultaneous sampling of lower limb, trunk, and upper limb musculature. This would be synchronized with the data obtained from items 2-4 below.

2 — Three or more high speed (200+FPS) digital video cameras, synchronized together and with items 1, 3, and 4. At this frame rate and with appropriate shuttering, excellent quality images are possible. These images can be stored in computer files and then superimposed on the computer screen with the EMG data, along with grip and foot pressures data from items 3 and 4.

3 — One complete computerized unit to measure forces on the plantar surfaces of both feet, to be synchronized with items 1, 2 and 4.

4 — One complete computerized unit to measure grip pressures from both hands. (I've not seen such a unit, but the technology exists to create it).

5 — Computers sophisticated enough to handle the above requirements.

6 — Selected training devices for enhancing flexibility, instantaneous power, balance, and so on, as well as devices for measuring these parameters.

7 — A laboratory of sufficient size to house items 1-6, with all the necessary electronic equipment and software to measure clubhead characteristics prior to and during contact.

The above list represents the important items necessary to equip such a laboratory, and would permit researchers a great opportunity to add significantly to both our knowledge and, perhaps more importantly, our ability to teach the skills and enhance the playing ability and satisfaction of golfers. Perhaps one day in the near future, these labs will be commonplace, and will be part of each golfer's quest for improved playing ability.

A Last Word

And so we come to the end of the reading portion of the experimenter's guide to the full golf swing. I hope that for the reader the fun has just begun. Approach your golf pro, or a patient and knowledgeable friend, get yourself a video camera, and head for the driving range. Explore that unique combination of tissues that separates you from the rest of humanity, and experiment. There is a more repeatable and efficient full golf swing within, and I hope that this book can help you discover it.

Enjoy the journey.

Appendix

Abdominals

Contraindicated

- Emphasis on hip flexors
- Strains on lumbar vertebrae

- Trunk OFF Ground - unnecessary strain on Lumbar Discs

- Full sit-up not needed for abdominal training

Safer Options (Isometrics Held for 10 seconds – 3 repetitions)

- Isometric contractions – normal standing posture

- Abdominals contracting isometrically to hold position

- Ball supports lumbar lordotic curve-isometric contraction

Trunk Extensors (Back Muscles)

Contraindicated

- Excessive lumbar flexion
- No significant stretch effect

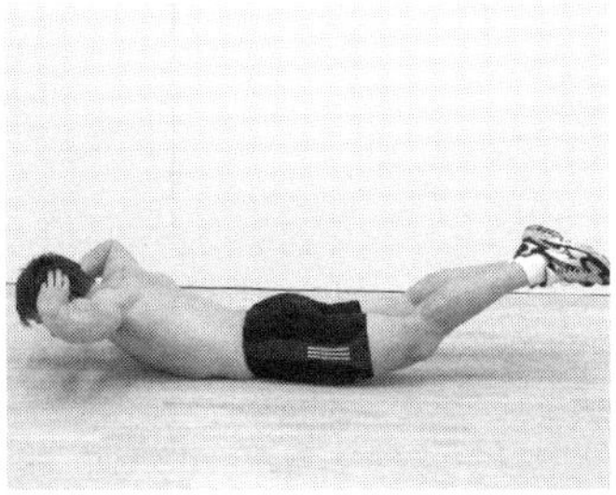

- Excessive compressive forces on lumbar vertebrae

- Excessive compressive forces on lumbar vertebrae

Hip & Thigh Musculature

Contraindicated

- Excessive loading on knees during eccentric landing (cruciate ligaments, menisci)

- Excessive compression and shearing on menisci

- Less knee strain, may bother lumbar area

Trunk Rotators

Contraindicated

- Excessive moment arm
- Dangerous torque at most speeds

- Excessive trunk torque
- Knee structures vulnerable

- Performed slowly – less dangerous

Safer Option

- Smaller moment arm
- Perform slowly

Upper Body Musculature

Contraindicated

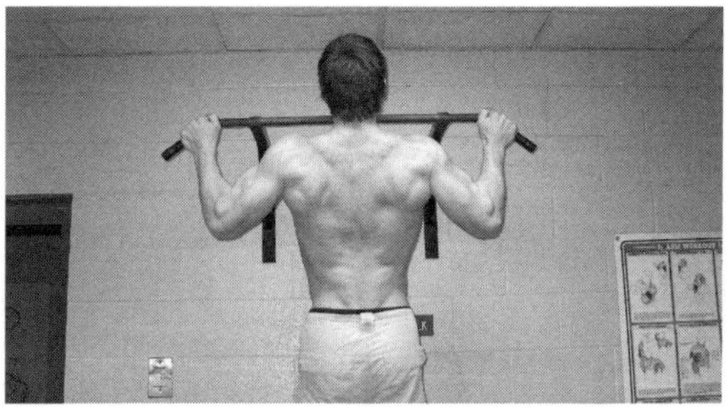

- Excessive resistance for most golfers

- Any prolonged hanging problematic
- Particularly with lower body twisting added

Shoulder Joint Abductors

Contraindicated

- Extra resistance unnecessary
  Possible impingement

Safer Option

- Arm weight only

Chest Musculature

Contraindicated

- Full body weight unnecessary

Safer Option

- Decrease moment arm
- Add mat under knees for comfort

Aerobics

Contraindicated

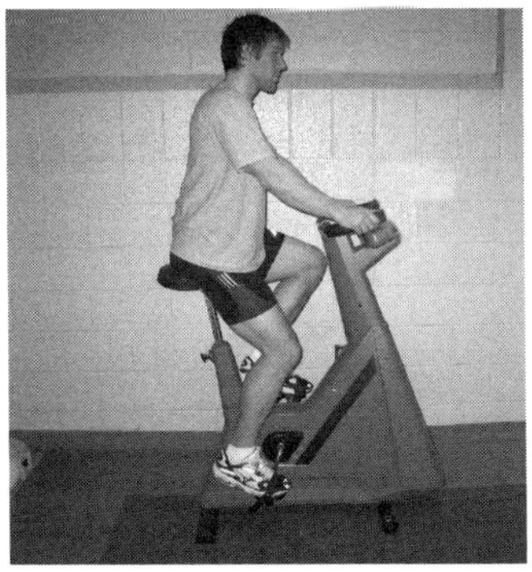

- Causes hamstrings and hip flexors to become tighter

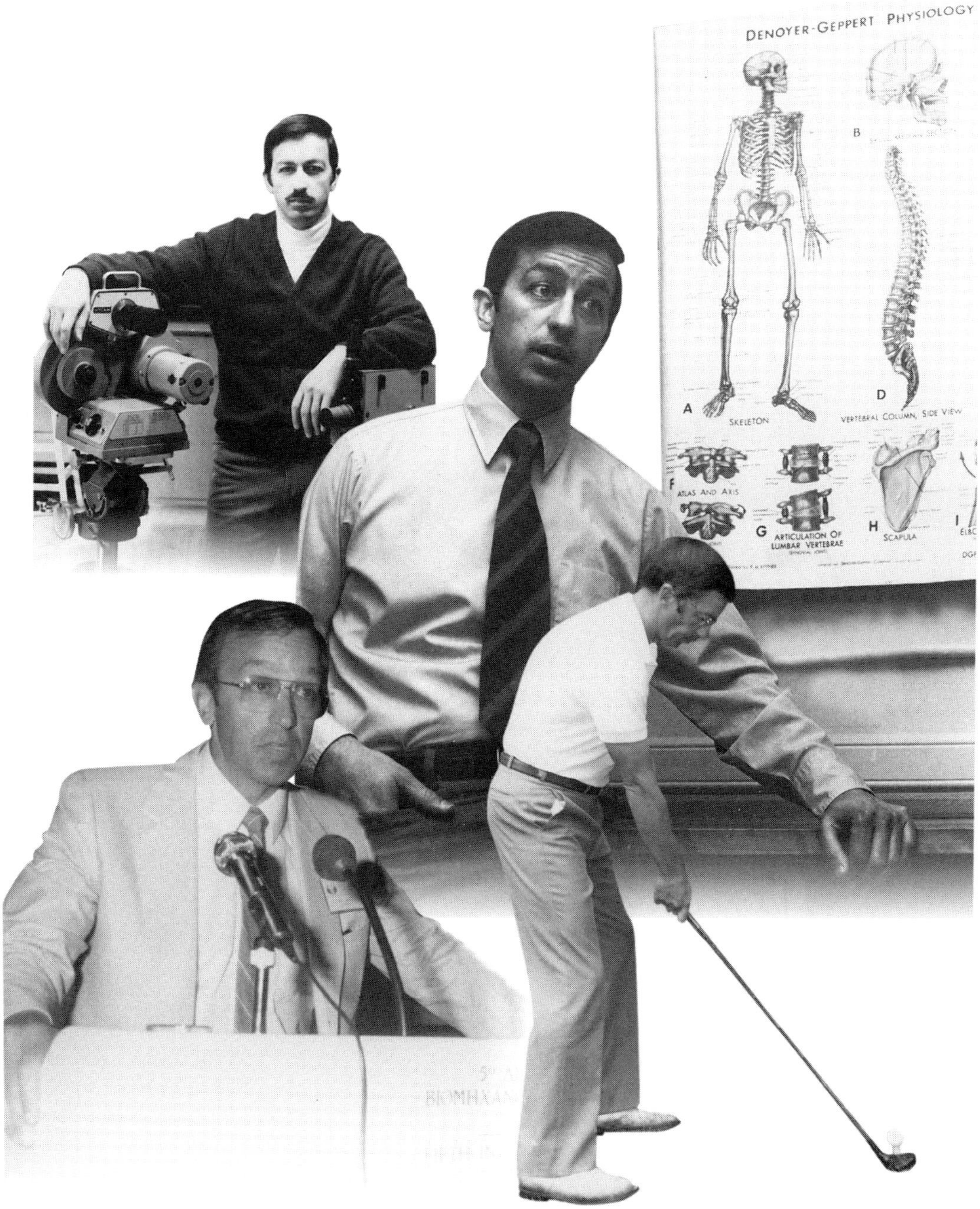
DENOYER-GEPPERT PHYSIOLOGY
A
SKELETON
B
D
VERTEBRAL COLUMN, SIDE VIEW
F
ATLAS AND AXIS
G
ARTICULATION OF
LUMBAR VERTEBRAE
H
SCAPULA
I

Résumé

L. E. Holt, PhD

Dr. Larry Holt is Full Professor of Kinesiology in the School of Health and Human Performance, Dalhousie University, and Adjunct Professor, St. Francis Xavier University. He, together with his graduate students and research associates, has published over 100 papers (excluding abstracts) in the fields of Sport and Exercise Sciences. In addition, he has made 143 scholarly presentations at numerous Learned Societies and Sport Associations, 70 being international.

His research has been featured nationally on Hockey Night in Canada (10 programs), Canadian Football League telecasts (3 programs), Marketplace and numerous radio and other TV programs. He has served as a consultant to the Canadian Military (twice), Canadian Curling Association, Canadian Swimming Association, Canadian Amateur Football Association, the Calgary Flames, Quebec Nordiques, and Minnesota North Stars. His most recent consultancy has been with the Association in Defense of the Wrongly Convicted (AIDWYC) in its successful overturning of the guilty verdict in the Clayton Johnson case.

He is known internationally for his book, *Scientific Stretching for Sport – 3S* (1973), which was the first to adapt PNF principles to flexibility training for athletics. He has invented three exercise related devices, one of which is patented. He is Past President of the International Society of Biomechanics in Sports (ISBS), and is listed in *Canadian Who's Who*.

In addition to his academic work in Sport/Exercise Science, he has competed in numerous sports throughout his life, achieving his greatest success in swimming, having won the New England AAU outdoor 200 meter Individual Medley Championship in 1959, and setting four Masters swim records in Canada at ages 43 and 46. Golf is presently one of his primary interests both academically and as a participant.